Tough Guys
and Gals
of the Movies

Other movie books by Edward Edelson:

GREAT MONSTERS OF THE MOVIES
VISIONS OF TOMORROW
FUNNY MEN OF THE MOVIES
GREAT MOVIE SPECTACULARS

Tough Guys and Gals of the Movies

EDWARD EDELSON

DOUBLEDAY & COMPANY, INC., GARDEN CITY, NEW YORK

Library of Congress Cataloging in Publication Data
Edelson, Edward, 1932–
Tough guys and gals of the movies.
SUMMARY: A look at the traditional "bad guys" and
gals from the movies with special emphasis on the
careers of Humphrey Bogart, James Cagney, and Edward G.
Robinson.
1. Moving-picture actors and actresses—
United States—Biography—Juvenile literature.
[1. Motion picture actors and actresses] I. Title.
PN1998.A2E29   791.43′028′0922 [B] [920]
ISBN 0-385-12788-x Trade
      0-385-12789-8 Prebound
Library of Congress Catalog Card Number 77–17002

CONTENTS

Tough Guys
and Gals
of the Movies

THE MALTESE FALCON

In the center, the Black Bird. From left to right, Humphrey
Bogart, Peter Lorre, Mary Astor and Sydney Greenstreet.
(*Warner Brothers, 1941*)

Varieties of Tough

An excellent place to start a book on the tough guys of the movies is smack in the middle of *The Maltese Falcon,* the 1941 detective story that was directed by John Huston.

One reason for starting here is that many movie critics believe that *The Maltese Falcon* is the best detective movie ever made. Even today it shows up regularly in revival movie houses and on television, where it seems as fresh as ever. And almost every private-eye film made since then has been influenced by *The Maltese Falcon.* But we're interested in the movie because of the marvelous gallery of tough guys you can find in it—just about a complete cross-section of all the tough guys you'll find in films.

Start with Humphrey Bogart as Sam Spade, the hero of the film. He's got problems. His partner, Miles Archer, has been shot down. A man named Thursby, who Archer was supposed to tail, has also been killed. The cops think Sam Spade might have done either killing, and they're leaning on him. He's also getting some pressure from the woman who hired Miles Archer. She started off by saying that her name was Wonderly, but it turns out to be Brigid O'Shaughnessy. She runs around in tough company. There's the perfumed little dandy who carries a gun (Peter Lorre), the fat man with a rumbling laugh (Sydney Greenstreet), and the fat man's gunman (Elisha Cook, Jr.). They're all pretty tough.

So are the two detectives (Ward Bond and Barton MacLane) who are after Sam Spade. But he's just a little too smart and a little too fast for them. Sam Spade may get caught in tight corners, he may be beaten up, he may seem to bend or even break the law. But you know he'll get out of this mess intact, because he's tougher than everyone he's up against.

That makes Sam Spade the model of the Hollywood tough guy so many kids in those days tried to imitate. He might have been a detective, a cowboy, an aviator or what have you, but he was tough—slow to anger, controlled in his speech, steady of eye, quick of fist (or of gun) when needed.

Let's move on to Peter Lorre. In *The Maltese Falcon,* he's Joel Cairo, an oily little man with a peculiar accent and pretensions to toughness. He has crookedness on his mind, but somehow you doubt that he has whatever it takes to succeed at crime. It's a role that Peter Lorre was to play over and over. The movies also have many imitation Peter Lorres.

And Sydney Greenstreet, the fat man. Even today he is being imitated in television commercials and the like. He's smooth and cultivated. He offers you the best of cigars and the finest of drinks. He travels first class and is unfailingly polite. But you have the uneasy impression that if it was necessary, he would cut your throat for a quarter—or a shilling if the scene was London, or a franc in Paris.

Not that Sydney Greenstreet would do anything as crude as cutting a throat himself. He's too sophisticated for that. Instead, he'd turn the job over to a hired hand, like the young punk Wilmer, played by Elisha Cook, Jr. Unhappily, Wilmer is not too good at his job. At one point, Sam Spade takes Wilmer's gun away with very little effort. Even though Wilmer gets revenge of a sort by kicking Sam in the face, that happens only after Sam is given a drugged drink by the fat man. Wilmer is decidedly unimportant.

When the showdown comes, the fat man and Sam can discuss quite calmly the merits of framing Wilmer for a murder, even though the gunman is standing right there, rather helplessly. The weak-jawed, gun-toting hired hand of the kind played by Elisha Cook, Jr., shows up in many movies. Generally, he comes to a no-good end; any time a thrill is needed, he can be rubbed out with no great loss to the plot. That's what happens to a tough guy who isn't tough enough.

Then there are the cops. They're tough, too, but not

as tough as they might be because they depend too much on their badges for protection. Sam Spade knows that they can make life difficult for him, but he also knows that he's a shade too clever to let that happen. One way or another, the private eye can stay a step ahead of the cops. He may have to take a right to the jaw now and then without hitting back, but it's worth it to have the last laugh.

Finally, there's Brigid O'Shaughnessy, played by Mary Astor. She's a tough lady She can cry when she has to or seem as soft as butter, but there's toughness underneath. She's playing her own game, and Sam Spade needs a different kind of toughness to keep ahead of her.

That's the cast of characters, and it should be a familiar one to you. *The Maltese Falcon* may be an old movie, but the new films haven't broken very far away from the types of toughness in it. For example, some thirty-five years later, in a movie called *The Late Show,* Art Carney played a character who was pretty clearly Sam Spade all over again, with the years gone by letting him show his age. Carney's private eye has a hearing aid, a pot belly, a bad leg and maybe a bleeding ulcer.

The crooks are dressed in the best 1970s California Mod styles, and they speak in the slang of today. The girl, played by Lily Tomlin, is kookie in the fashion of the 1970s, and so she's hard to figure out. But the game is still the same, played with life and death and money and flying lead. And the private eye, Sam Spade almost at the age of Social Security, is still just a shade too tough for the bad guys.

It isn't quite the same as it was when *The Maltese Falcon* was made. Hollywood has changed. The studios used to turn out a flood of movies, and there was plenty of room for an army of tough guys and gals of varying kinds. You could see the same faces in film after film, playing different roles but putting on essentially the same show. Today, the flood of films has become a trickle. Television has taken away the audience that the films once had. But television doesn't have the same opportunity for tough guys and gals; there just isn't that much individuality to the faces on the tube.

The surprising thing is that the old Hollywood tough tradition continues so well. The old movies stubbornly refuse to fade away. The personalities from those movies are still very much with us. Bogart hasn't been on earth for many years, but his lisp and other mannerisms are still familiar to us. Sydney Greenstreet's fat man seems to show up in a surprising number of television shows and movie thrillers, although the modern imitators don't pack the same punch as the original did.

Indeed, to anyone who knows the old movies of Hollywood, an awful lot of the stuff that is supposed to be brand new seems to be an imitation of one sort or another. And so, let us go back and look over the originals, the tough guys of the movies who established the tradition that continues today. When you consider just how many people are making a living doing imitations, it's a good idea to examine the originals.

CASABLANCA

Bogart pours the champagne for Ingrid Bergman
while Dooley Wilson, as Sam, plays it again.
(*Warner Brothers, 1942*)

The Toughest of Them All

Of all the tough guys, would-be tough guys and not-quite tough guys who have paraded across the screen, three stand out as unique: Humphrey Bogart, Edward G. Robinson and James Cagney. Between them they seem to have pretty much cornered the market, partly because of their sheer durability. Over the years Bogart, Robinson and Cagney played so many different parts that, among them, they covered just about every possibility: good guys, bad guys, guys in between. Remember, those were the years when Hollywood was grinding out movies on an assembly line. It wasn't unusual for a star to make three or four movies in a single year. In that frantic era quantity seemed a lot more important than quality. Sometimes, if you see a lot of the films of the 1930s in a bunch, you get the impression that you're just seeing the same film over again. In those days Hollywood seemed to have a limited number of plots that were recycled to provide the necessary variety: first in the Big City, then in the South Seas, then in a cowboys-and-Indians Western, then in a prison saga, and so on ad infinitum.

In that kind of atmosphere the stars who made it weren't selling acting ability as much as they were selling sheer personality. One of the comforting things about going to the movies in those days was the knowledge that regardless of the plot, there would be the same familiar personalities on the screen. And make no mistake about it, Bogart, Robinson and Cagney had plenty of personality. It is personality that jumps out at you today the same as it did many years ago when the films were first made. One tribute to that old Hollywood kind of personality is the fact that comedians are still doing imitations of Bogart, Robinson and Cagney— and that the audience still laughs with recognition. It's worth looking closely at actors who can create that kind of recognition over a barrier of years and of different eras.

BOGART

Humphrey Bogart started in the movies in 1930, after a career on the stage. But he didn't make it. After a few lackluster films, he was let go by his studio and went back East. What made him a success was the Broadway production of *The Petrified Forest,* a play by Robert Sherwood, in which Bogart played the part of Duke Mantee. The play was a melodrama about a brief encounter between a doomed poet and a young girl at a desert luncheonette, but Bogart stood out as Duke, the gangster who was on the run from the cops, was obviously doomed, and who represented the lost, wild freedom of the American West.

Bogart came back to Hollywood in 1936 to play Duke Mantee in the film version of *The Petrified Forest,* which also starred Leslie Howard and Bette Davis. His success launched his Hollywood career for good—although it took a long, long time for Bogart really to hit the top. Today, when we remember Bogart as one of the greatest stars in Hollywood history, it's hard to recall the years when he played minor parts, often as the villain in rather cheap gangster movies or even Westerns. Would you believe Humphrey Bogart as a Mexican bandit who was trying to steal a gold shipment from Randolph Scott? So he was, in a film called *Virginia City.* How about Bogart as the Western villain fighting James Cagney, both of them looking out of place in Stetson hats and chaps (*The Oklahoma Kid*). In most of these films, Bogart's role usually ended when he was gunned down, either by the hero or by the cops. The last you saw of him was when he slumped to the ground, a pained look on his face, his hands clenched over his stomach (Hollywood wounds somehow never bled in those days). Occasionally, Bogart would have the brief triumph of doing dirt to the hero (as he did to Cagney in *The Roaring Twenties*), but you knew it couldn't last. Sooner or later he would get his comeuppance.

The Maltese Falcon broke Bogart out of that rut. For one thing, it allowed him to play a good (but tough) guy. That wasn't unique in his career. He had, for example, played the good-guy District Attorney who persuaded that shady lady, Bette Davis, to turn honest in *Marked Woman.* But *The Maltese Falcon* also showed that Bogart had that elusive thing called star quality, the quality that brought him good leading roles.

One such role, a part that is regarded as one of the high points in Bogart's career, was the portrayal of the ex-convict in *High Sierra,* which appeared the same year as *The Maltese Falcon.* The character played by Bogart in the film was as tough as nails. He could send a chill down your back when he tapped his fingernail on a tabletop to show how a few slugs from a tommygun had wiped out another hood. But he could also pay for an operation to repair the deformed foot of a winsome young girl, played by Joan Leslie. Like Duke Mantee, the Bogart character in *High Sierra* was doomed. He was hunted down, trapped in the mountains that gave the movie its name, and killed. But the audience could sense that this seemingly ruthless killer was a human being who somehow could be pitied. It was a triumph of the Bogart personality.

The next high point in Bogart's career—*the* high point, many fans believe—came in 1943 with *Casablanca.* Viewed logically, *Casablanca* is sentimental trash. Every character in the film is, in one way or an-

other, a cliché. Bogart is Rick, the tough, laconic soldier of fortune who (of course) turns out to be sentimental at the core. Peter Lorre is the sniveling criminal
who is trying to be in Rick's class and not making it.
("I don't mind a parasite," Bogart tells Lorre, "but I do
mind a cut-rate one.") Sydney Greenstreet is the chuck-
ling fat man again, this time in a tarboosh. Ingrid Bergman is the lady with a past (who, of course, did it all
for love). Conrad Veidt is the ruthless Nazi; Claude
Rains the cynical French policeman; S. Z. Sakall is the
jowly, comic-relief waiter at Rick's night club—and on
and on, the whole Hollywood stock company assembled
to do the usual routines.

But it all works so beautifully that you forget the
clichés. Casablanca just about swept the Academy
Awards that year—for its witty script, for its director,
for best movie. Bogart didn't win an Oscar, but he established a legend. Thirty years later, Woody Allen
could grab audiences both on stage and on the screen
by playing the Bogart fantasy role in *Play It Again,
Sam,* to audiences consisting mostly of people who
hadn't been born when *Casablanca* was made (and
who were generally unaware that Rick never did say,
"Play it again, Sam" to his side-kick in the movie).

Oh, that Bogart legend—Bogie, the tough guy with
the built-in curl in his lip and his semi-lisp (caused by
an accident when he was a baby), the man who could
look chaos in the eye, who could meet corruption with
honor and danger with a laugh and always come out
the winner. A generation of teen-agers grew up trying
to live the Bogie legend, and the fact that campus

screens keep showing Bogart revivals indicates that the legend still is alive in these unsentimental days.

The legend grew when Bogart met Lauren Bacall, whom he was to marry. Their first film, in 1944, was *To Have and Have Not,* a screen version of a Hemingway story. Their second was *The Big Sleep,* a detective story by Raymond Chandler. Bogie was perfect for both parts. He was the perfect actor to play the tough-yet-tender Hemingway hero, and he was made to order as Philip Marlowe, the detective against whom just about all tough private eyes are measured.

You can win a trivia bet easily by challenging someone to name the seven actors who have played Philip Marlowe on the screen (answer: George Montgomery, Bogart, Robert Montgomery, Dick Powell, James Garner, Elliott Gould, Robert Mitchum). People mostly remember Bogart in the role because he made it so much his own.

The legend lived on even though Bogart had about as many misses as hits during the rest of his career. Two high spots are unforgettable: Bogart as Fred C. Dobbs, the rundown American drifter in Mexico who is torn apart by suspicion and paranoia after a gold strike, in *The Treasure of the Sierra Madre,* one of the best films ever to come out of Hollywood. And Bogart as Charlie Allnut, goaded by Katharine Hepburn into a funny kind of nobility as they fought their way down an African river to attack a German gunboat in *The African Queen.* Bogart won the Oscar for *The African Queen,* as much for sentimental reasons as for the acting he did. Truth to tell, he never was regarded as a great actor. But he was—and is—regarded as a great legend, a personality against whom few could stand comparison, a tough guy just about in a league of his own. That was Bogie.

ROBINSON

Like Bogart, Edward G. Robinson came snarling onto the screen as a gangster, and it was the kind of part that he was to play often as the years went by. Robinson's fame was made when he appeared as *Little Caesar* in Mervyn LeRoy's gangster film of 1931. The tough, stocky little man with a unique way of drawling out his "Yeah," Robinson never could have the sheer physical appeal of Bogart. For one thing, he wasn't really very handsome. You could never imagine women getting carried away with Edward G. Robinson the way they were with Bogie. Robinson's kind of attraction came from the sheer power he radiated. From the moment he came on the screen as a hired hand in *Little Caesar,* you knew that Robinson was going to fight his way to the top, no matter who he had to rub out. When he was shot down in the street and gasped out his famous last words, "Mother of God, is this the end of Rico?" you felt that only bullets could stop his insatiable drive for power.

Many actors would have stayed in the successful rut of the kind that Robinson abandoned. Yes, he played many gangsters, but he also got the chance to prove that he was an actor of impressive versatility. By 1935,

Robinson could even make something of a joke out of his *Little Caesar* image when, in *The Whole Town's Talking,* he played a double role—not only a gangster on the loose, but also the meek little bank clerk who had the bad luck to look like the hoodlum. In *A Slight Case of Murder,* made three years later, he played a gangster for laughs again. In that film, Robinson was Marco, a brewery owner who had prospered during Prohibition but was having tough times when he had to compete legitimately after Repeal, whose daughter was about to marry a state policeman, and who had the additional problem of clearing out a roomful of dead bodies left to him after someone else's holdup. It was a comedy, so everything came out right for Marco in the end.

More variety: Robinson as an American agent in *Confessions of a Nazi Spy,* one of the first anti-Nazi movies; Robinson playing the title part in *Dr. Ehrlich's Magic Bullet,* a biography of a celebrated nineteenth-century scientist; Robinson as the all-seeing insurance investigator who steadily tracked down a killer, not knowing that it was his best friend (Fred MacMurray), in the chilling *Double Indemnity* of 1944; Robinson as the Nazi hunter on the trail of mass murderer Orson Welles, an escaped Nazi who had found refuge in a peaceful New England village (*The Stranger,* 1946). Then, for old times, he was the *Little Caesar* character again, appearing with Humphrey Bogart and Lauren Bacall in *Key Largo.* In that 1948 movie, Robinson was the heavy and Bogart the hero who beat the bad guys despite a hurricane and heavy odds against him.

LITTLE CAESAR
Edward G. Robinson strikes a classic pose.
(*First National, 1931*)

Bogart had died young, almost at the peak of his fame. Robinson kept on acting, in good films and in bad. There was a run of rather second-rate gangster films in the 1950s, a good snarling villain's role in Cecil B. DeMille's garish production of *The Ten Commandments,* and then a little bit of everything: a middle-aged businessman in love in *Middle of the Night* (1956), a government official in the pro-Indian western, *Cheyenne Autumn* (1964), a jungle smuggler in the exciting African story, *A Boy Ten Feet Tall* (1965), and so on. His last role was in a science-fiction movie of no great distinction, *Soylent Green,* released in 1973. He died the next year, just before he could receive the Oscar that had been voted to him for the work of his lifetime.

It was impressive work. The brash young tough guy of *Little Caesar* had proved that his acting range was surprisingly broad. He could be a gangster, a scientist, a clerk and a detective with equal conviction. There is no Edward G. Robinson cult to rival Bogart's but Robinson left a huge legacy of films that will be giving pleasure to audiences for many years to come.

CAGNEY

Bogart came slouching onto the screen. Robinson came swaggering onto the screen. It's not much of an exaggeration to say that James Cagney came dancing onto the screen.

At first glance, that seems to be an unlikely description. Cagney's film success started with *The Public Enemy,* the 1931 film in which he played a tough Chicago kid who fights his way to the top of a bootlegging operation, using fists and guns freely, breaking his poor mother's heart and eventually being gunned down and dumped lifeless on his own doorstep. The scene most people remember from *The Public Enemy*—one of the most famous scenes ever made in Hollywood— has Cagney shoving a grapefruit in the face of Mae Clarke, the moll who had displeased him by some carping remarks at breakfast. So why think of this little fighting guttersnipe as a dancer?

Because Cagney was, in fact, a dancer to begin with. He began in show business as a song-and-dance man. His first film featured him in that role. And he was naturally graceful. Even as a gangster, he had a lithe grace that was as distinctive as his fast, clipped speech. Cagney went on from *The Public Enemy* to play a series of tough-guy roles in which he was rough on women, but the dancer part of him was always there. It surfaced in 1933 when he starred in *Footlight Parade,* as a producer of musicals, in which he did get to do some dancing.

A tough guy who could dance? That was only part of the story. It soon developed that Cagney was a tough guy who could not only dance but could also be funny, and a few things more. In 1935 (the same year that he played a tough guy on the right side of the law in *G Men*), Cagney played the part of Bottom in a Warner Brothers production of Shakespeare's *A Midsummer Night's Dream.* Three years later, he was a

THE PUBLIC ENEMY

James Cagney demonstrates his disapproval of Mae Clarke,
in a scene that no one ever forgot.
(*Warner Brothers, 1931*)

wise-cracking screen writer in *Boy Meets Girl,* a farce that made ample fun of the screwball, anything-goes Hollywood atmosphere of that era. That same year (Hollywood turned out films in quantity at that time), he was a no-good who went to the electric chair in *Angels With Dirty Faces,* but who won the audience's heart because he put on a sniveling act so that the slum kids who worshiped him wouldn't think he was a hero. Incidentally, Bogart played a shyster lawyer in that film.

It was in *Angels With Dirty Faces* that Cagney used the mannerisms that comedians still imitate today, bouncing on the balls of his feet while he held his elbows tightly at his side. He explained later that he had copied some of the characters from the New York East Side where he grew up. However, Cagney didn't sneer, "You dirty rat," in *Angels With Dirty Faces.* In fact, he never said it at all in any of his screen appearances, even though everyone seems to think he did.

Cagney got an Academy Award nomination for *Angels With Dirty Faces.* He soon made two more outstanding gangster films, *Each Dawn I Die* and *The Roaring Twenties.* But it was fitting that when he did win an Oscar, it was as a song-and-dance man, in *Yankee Doodle Dandy,* the 1942 film biography of James M. Cohan. World War II had just begun, and it was just the right atmosphere for this (literally) flag-waving story of Cohan, perhaps the greatest song-and-dance man in American history. Cagney played the part to the hilt, and danced up a storm to boot. It was probably the high point of his career.

There were a few more high points. One of them was *White Heat,* the 1949 film in which Cagney played Cody Jarrett, a psychopathic mamma's boy who went berserk in prison when he heard the news of his mother's death. *White Heat* ended with one of the most terrifying scenes of all: Cagney on top of a gas tank, shrieking, "Top of the world, ma, top of the world," before the tank ignited and seared him in a sheet of flame.

Cagney also did an excellent job in the film version of *Mister Roberts,* playing the unsympathetic role of a nasty, small-minded ship's captain who thwarted Henry Fonda's wishes to get into combat. Then there was *One, Two, Three,* Billy Wilder's film about a Coca-Cola executive suffering through some farcical moments in the Berlin of the Cold War years. *One, Two, Three* was a nonstop farce that ranks as one of Cagney's best parts, a film that showed just how good a comedian he was. It was also the last role he played on film. Without any particular regret and with his talents still in demand, the little tough guy walked away from the movies to live comfortably in retirement on a New York farm. It was a happy ending.

Good Guys, Bad Guys, Tough Guys and Nice Guys

What makes a tough guy a tough guy? That isn't as easy to answer as might appear at first. Take the case of John Wayne. The movie that made him famous, after years of Grade-B Westerns, was *Stagecoach,* now regarded as a classic, which John Ford directed in 1939. In *Stagecoach,* Wayne played the Ringo Kid, who was fresh out of prison. Before the film ended, the Kid would be in a shoot-it-out showdown in which plenty of blood would flow.

Over the years, John Wayne has made many, many movies, in which he has been handy with both his fists and with guns. Just about every one of those films has featured at least one all-out fist fight and a lot of shooting. On film, John Wayne has beat up or shot down an almost uncountable number of men. Yet somehow, you never think of John Wayne as a tough guy, in the way that you think of Cagney or Robinson or Bogart as tough guys. Rather, you get the impression that he's a nice guy who rather reluctantly has to be tough.

It's hard to say why, but there is that core of niceness in the John Wayne screen character. If you look at the long list of film parts he has played, you'll be struck by one thing: John Wayne has almost never played a bad guy, at least not in his mature years. Maybe the closest he came to it was in another Western classic, this one directed by Howard Hawks, *Red River*. Wayne plays Tom Dunson, a driven man whose fiancée is killed in an Indian attack and who adopts a young boy, played by Montgomery Clift. Most of the movie is devoted to an epic trail drive. Dunson must get not only his cattle but those of his neighbors to market to save the ranch he has built up over the years.

Goaded by Dunson's harsh, unyielding discipline, the trail hands rebel, and Montgomery Clift takes over the drive. Riding away, Dunson swears bitterly that he will come back with murder in his heart. If it were Bogart or Cagney or Robinson you might believe it. But with John Wayne, you have the feeling that a happy ending will result. It does. Wayne and Clift are reconciled at the end (by the love of a woman), an outcome that possibly only John Wayne can prevent from being mawkish.

Considering that he was never regarded as a great actor, John Wayne made a surprisingly large number of great or near-great movies. Many of them were under the direction of John Ford, who is generally regarded as the best director of Westerns on the American screen. In those John Ford Westerns, you can see Wayne aging gradually, yet never betraying his basic screen character.

In *Fort Apache,* a John Ford film built around a rigid, paranoid commanding officer who leads his men to slaughter in an Indian ambush, it is Henry Fonda, normally a good guy, who plays the heavy. John Wayne is the level-headed second-in-command who does what he can to prevent the massacre and then gallantly protects the legend of the dead man for the good of the army—a scenario that is disturbingly reminiscent of the story of General George Custer.

It has been said that John Wayne is the only real Western hero, and that one way or another, anyone who plays the hero in a Western is imitating him, consciously or otherwise. Whether that is true or not, it cannot be denied that Wayne dominates the modern Western, by the sheer number and variety of parts he has played for Ford and many other directors. And yet many critics believe that his very best role was in a film set in Ireland—*The Quiet Man,* in which Wayne plays an American who has come to a small Irish village, haunted by his past (it would be unfair to give away that part of the plot). Maureen O'Hara is perfect as the colleen with whom Wayne falls in love; the long and spectacular fight between Wayne and Victor McLaglen may be the best ever put on film; and the photography is John Ford's unforgettable tribute to the beauty of Ireland.

Unfortunately, more people seem to remember

Wayne for two considerably poorer films—*The Alamo,* a bloated version of the gallant episode in the history of Texas, and *True Grit,* in which Wayne's part seems to be more a travesty of his usual role than anything else. Both of those pictures made money, and Wayne got his only Oscar for the Rooster Cogburn role in *True Grit,* but it seems certain that Wayne will be better remembered over the long run for many of the other parts he played.

What is true of John Wayne is also true of other stars who are or were prominent in Westerns. Gary Cooper, for example, hardly ever played any character that could be called a bad guy. There was no question of Cooper's toughness; in many a Western he faced the villains and either outslugged them or outshot them. But, as was true of John Wayne, you always had the feeling that Gary Cooper never enjoyed the shooting as Bogart or Cagney or Robinson gave the impression of doing.

In one of Cooper's most memorable roles, the beleaguered sheriff in *High Noon,* there came a time when he put his head down and wept from sheer frustration and loneliness. The fact that Cooper thereupon took up his gun and went out and killed the bad men couldn't erase that moment. Could you imagine Bogart shedding that kind of tears?

Another measure of Cooper's nice-guy status was his ability to switch easily to comedy roles. He was, in fact, one of the most successful stars of the screwball comedies of the 1930s and 1940s. He generally played two kinds of roles. For Frank Capra, a director who specialized in comedies in which an unsophisticated good guy

TRUE GRIT
John Wayne, true to his image of the tough guy who
could also be tender, looks after Kim Darby.
(*Paramount, 1969*)

managed to overcome the city slickers (cynics called it Capra-corn), Cooper was the "Aw, shucks, ma" character; the films include *Mr. Deeds Goes to Town* and *Meet John Doe*. The audiences had their handkerchiefs out half the time and guffawed the other half.

For a number of other directors, Cooper played the suave, sophisticated hero of drawing-room dramas—you could say that in these films he was the kind of city slicker who was the villain in the Capra movies. It was a tribute to the Cooper magnetism, and to his acting, that he could shift so easily from the cow-town saloon to the small-town parlor to the Fifth Avenue penthouse. Maybe the best of the latter roles came toward the end of his career, in *Love in the Afternoon,* a 1957 comedy in which he was the rich, experienced man of the world who was captured in the end by the shy, inexperienced Audrey Hepburn. To the end, Cooper was the kind of good guy who couldn't break that girl's heart.

Much the same is true of James Stewart, who also had the facility of moving from the saddle to just plain folks roles to sophisticated comedy. But there was more toughness in Stewart than there was in Cooper, or at least in the characters they played. In many of Stewart's Westerns, he played a man with a dark and bloody past; honest, now, but with sinister overtones remaining.

Perhaps his most typical role is in an underrated Western, *Bend of the River,* made in 1952. Stewart plays a gunman who is going to Oregon to start an honest life. He falls in with a wagon train of settlers who need food to get them through the first hard winter. Unfortunately, the man who sells them supplies won't deliver after a gold strike sends prices skyrocketing. Stewart first grabs the supplies away. Then, when dishonest wagon drivers dump him so they can sell the goods to the miners, Stewart relentlessly hunts them down, one man against a dozen, mercilessly killing them off until he recaptures the wagons. In the end, he gets acceptance by the farmers, but the viewer is left wondering whether this hard-as-nails man can settle down to a placid life.

Most of his fans would rather remember the softer Stewart of his earlier career—for example, the drawling, diffident sheriff of *Destry Rides Again,* a movie in which Stewart took up his guns only reluctantly, after all else had failed and the villains had treacherously gunned down his side-kick; *Mr. Smith Goes to Washington,* more Capra-corn, in which he is a country bumpkin who is made a U. S. Senator so the city slickers can use him (guess who wins out in the end); *You Can't Take It With You,* another Capra movie, in which he played the only level-headed member of a delightfully wacky family. In the end, the verdict on Stewart is: mostly a nice guy, but just those few hints of nasty toughness to unsettle the filmgoer.

As for Clark Gable, maybe the biggest star of all in the heyday of Hollywood, his toughness is all indoors. Significantly, Gable made hardly any Westerns at all. His typical tough-guy role was as a gambler, maybe a night-club owner, with a sharp eye for beautiful women. You always had the uneasy feeling that the deck of cards Gable was using might have been marked and that the roulette wheel seemed to lean suspiciously to one side. But you never had the feeling that he was eager to pull his gun and start shooting. There was even less of

DESTRY RIDES AGAIN

Marlene Dietrich doesn't seem to be having much success
at tempting good (but tough) guy James Stewart.
(*MGM, 1939*)

a feeling that Gable enjoyed gun fights and brawls, even though he could hold his own in any fight. He was always a man who could be reformed, even tamed, by the right kind of woman.

Errol Flynn, the great swashbuckler of Hollywood costume epics, was even more of a non-tough guy. Flynn made a long string of pirate films, historical melodramas and Westerns in which he was called on to be handy with sword, bow-and-arrow or gun, but he always seemed to have one eye on the heroine, or any other beautiful woman who was in sight. The movie that made him famous, *Captain Blood* (1935), pretty much set the pattern for the rest of his career.

As a seventeenth-century English doctor who is unjustly sold into slavery (yes, they could do that in those days) because he had treated some rebels against the king, Flynn first captures the heart of the daughter of the colonial governor. Then he outwits his captors, not only escaping but also taking most of his fellow prisoners with him—and, to top it all, capturing a sailing vessel that enables him to set up shop as a pirate. After all of that, it is possible to believe (at least in the darkness of the movie theater) that Flynn will kill his pirate rival in duel, get a pardon from the new king and be made governor of the colony where he was an exile—and, incidentally, win the heroine.

Captain Blood also set a pattern by having Basil Rathbone as a villain. In the years that followed, it seems that just about every swashbuckling movie that Flynn made ended with a long, spectacular and acrobatic duel between him and Rathbone. In the course of the duel, there always came a moment when the two would lock together, their faces a few inches apart, and hiss at each other something like "Norman dog!" "Saxon swine!"—after which Flynn would go on to polish off his opponent, who usually toppled picturesquely from a parapet, staircase, battlement or other grandiose height to his doom. The best swashbuckler that Flynn ever made—maybe the best that Hollywood ever made—was *The Adventures of Robin Hood* (1938), which still holds up very well and which, of course, had Basil Rathbone as one of the chief villains.

Alphabetically, Henry Fonda comes right after Errol Flynn. If anything, Fonda's screen character is even gentler than Flynn's. Errol Flynn could play General Custer (in *They Died With Their Boots On*), but Fonda could top that by being *Young Mr. Lincoln* in a 1939 biography. Nobility was Henry Fonda's hallmark. When he played the part of Wyatt Earp, the deadly Western lawman, in John Ford's *My Darling Clementine* (1946), it was made clear that he took the job only because the vicious Clanton family had killed his younger brother. And when he rubbed out the Clantons in the famous shoot-out at the O K Corral, it was obvious that he was doing it rather regretfully, in the way that a teacher punishes an unruly student.

Noble good guys have always been a Hollywood staple. But so have nasty, bad guys. Every hero needs a villain, and the movies have always been able to supply them. It's surprising how many actors have been able to build long and successful careers on their ability to be tough and villainous. Let's look at some of them.

It's Good
To Be Bad

"Hey, listen to this. This guy pushes a woman down the stairs in a wheelchair!"

That was the first startled reaction of a promising young actor named Richard Widmark when he read a movie script that had been offered to him. He took the part of a snarling, sadistic young punk named Tommy Udo in *Kiss of Death,* a 1947 movie, and was immediately launched on a career of screen villainy. Audiences especially loved (or hated) the nasty little giggle that marked Widmark as a particular no-good. He really did seem to be having a great time when he shoved little old ladies down staircases or otherwise rubbed out people.

The next year it was *The Street With No Name,* in which Widmark played the leader of a gang that was infiltrated by the good-guy, G-man Mark Stevens. After

KISS OF DEATH
Richard Widmark, nasty to the core, confronts Victor Mature.
(*20th Century-Fox, 1947*)

that it was *Yellow Sky,* in which he was a Western gunman who made trouble for Gregory Peck. Both of them were members of the same gang of bank robbers, but it was Gregory Peck who was won over to the right side by the influence of the heroine, Anne Baxter, and Widmark who insisted on stealing the gold that had been saved over the years by Anne's movie grandfather. Naturally, Widmark bit the dust.

Villainy pays. Widmark has had a long and fruitful screen career, during which he has played his share of good guys. For example, he was especially distinguished in *Panic in the Streets,* the 1950 film, directed by Elia Kazan, in which Widmark played a young Public Health Service doctor desperately trying to prevent a plague from breaking out in New Orleans.

He's been a hero in a number of Westerns, he's been on the right side of the law in many detective movies, he's even done some effective work in comedies. But the snarl, the sneer and the hard, cold eyes are always there when a villainous tough-guy part comes along. Over the years, Widmark has played such parts as the vicious bigot out to get Sidney Poitier in *No Way Out* (1950); a conceited killer in one episode of *O. Henry's Full House* (1952); a paranoid Navy officer who provokes a nuclear outbreak in *The Bedford Incident* (1965); and a cold-blooded gunslinger in *Alvarez Kelly* (1966).

Widmark's most notable recent villainy was in *Murder on the Orient Express,* the 1974 thriller based on the book by Agatha Christie. He was absolutely convincing as the swinish, brutal kidnap-murderer who richly deserves to be murdered in turn. It took the

Widmark sort of nastiness to create a character whose death was mourned by absolutely no one.

Pure villainy has always been a salable commodity in Hollywood, and many a career has been built on the ability to project almost undiluted badness. After all, being all bad is rather a rare skill. Someone like James Cagney couldn't do it. Even in Cagney's most unsympathetic appearances, such as the role of the psychopathic Cody Jarrett in *White Heat,* the audience still had the feeling that the killer was a human being. The gunman played by Humphrey Bogart in *High Sierra* was ruthless, but you could feel some sympathy for him. It isn't so for Widmark and other villains of his ilk. They draw people to the theater out of sheer nastiness.

The tradition goes back to Erich von Stroheim, the man with the sneering Prussian accent and the shaved head who was advertised as "the man you love to hate." Von Stroheim's story is one of the most fascinating in all of Hollywood history. He came to the United States before World War I and built a successful career as a screen actor by playing a series of roles in which he was a villainous German, often an army officer, usually a cad, swindler and worse. He went on from there to an almost unbelievable career as a movie director. Even though he had some successes, his penchant for shooting enormously long films and spending money lavishly drove studio heads to despair; eventually, his extravagance drove him out of the business.

Von Stroheim carried on as an actor, usually as a villain. One exception was the French-made *Grand Illusion,* one of the greatest war films ever made, in which he played the sympathetic role of an aristocratic

AS YOU DESIRE ME

Erich von Stroheim, every inch the man you love to hate.
The woman is Greta Garbo in a blond wig.
(*MGM, 1932*)

prison commander. When World War II came along, Von Stroheim was in great demand because he was able to make Nazis appear as brutal as they were in real life.

One of his best World War II appearances was as Field Marshall Erwin Rommel, the commander of the Afrika Korps, in *Five Graves to Cairo.* Foppishly carrying a tasseled fly-swatter, meticulously clipping off his words, cold-bloodedly discussing the coming Nazi take-over of the world, Von Stroheim was truly a man you loved to hate. (Just to show how quickly times changed, by 1951 Rommel was being portrayed as a sensitive anti-Nazi figure in *The Desert Fox,* which had James Mason playing quite a different Rommel from the one depicted by Von Stroheim.)

Von Stroheim's very last American film role was in *Sunset Boulevard,* the 1950 classic in which he played the present butler and former husband of a faded silent screen star, Gloria Swanson. It was essentially a sympathetic role, an illustration of the difficulty of remaining entirely villainous through a long career. Only now and then does an actor come along whose fans insist on nothing but bad-guy parts.

Dan Duryea was one of those rare characters. In a Hollywood career that lasted nearly thirty years, Duryea had only a few nice-guy parts, and his fans didn't like them. The people who bought movie tickets wanted to see Duryea in the kind of role that introduced him to Hollywood—the weak, sniveling and unscrupulous Cousin Leo in the 1941 film version of Lillian Hellman's play, *The Little Foxes.*

After that any time there was a defenseless woman to be beat up, a harmless bystander to be gunned down, or a hapless family man to be blackmailed, it was a job for Dan Duryea. As Bosley Crowther, film critic of the New York *Times,* wrote of Duryea's acting in a film called *The Woman in the Window,* "Dan Duryea is so good in the role of the blackmailer that you actually feel like hissing him." (Incidentally, it was Edward G. Robinson who was being blackmailed in this 1945 movie.)

Two years earlier Duryea had played a good guy in the wartime movie *Sahara,* in which he was Humphrey Bogart's side-kick. It just didn't go over. In 1946 Duryea tried his hand at comedy, playing a butler who pretended to be master of the house while the boss was away in *White Tie and Tails.* The film flopped. It was no use explaining that Duryea in real life was a devoted family man and a pleasant man who was interested in gardening.

His fans wanted to see him in things like *Along Came Jones,* a mostly comic Western starring Gary Cooper in which Duryea played a gunman so psychopathic that his own girl friend eventually shot him, or in films like *Scarlet Street, Johnny Stool Pigeon,* or *The Underworld Story.* When he socked Joan Bennett on the chin in *The Woman in the Window,* the fan mail came pouring in, most of it quite admiring. His fellow professionals admired him as an actor who always did a workmanlike job, no matter how villainous the role might be.

Another actor whose career had almost nothing but

SCARLET STREET
Dan Duryea being cheap and mean in his own inimitable style.
(*Universal, 1946*)

bad-guy roles was Barton MacLane, a burly man who always seemed to play a heavy whose name was something like Blacky, and who always lost the big fist fight with the hero. If you remember, we first met Barton MacLane as one of the cops in *The Maltese Falcon*. True to his screen destiny, he was the unsympathetic cop in that film, the one who was pushing Sam Spade just a little too hard and who took an unjustified swing at the hero. That was pretty much the story of his life on film: always the bad guy.

MacLane got into movies in the marvelously casual way that was typical of bygone Hollywood. He was a football player at Wesleyan University in 1924 and ran back a kickoff for a touchdown. Pretty soon he was acting in *The Quarterback,* a film starring Richard Dix. It was only after that first film appearance that MacLane started studying acting. He was in some Broadway plays ("probably the brawniest actor on the New York stage today," one newspaper wrote of him at the time) before returning to Hollywood for a long string of films with titles like *Black Fury, Captain Scarface, Gunfighters of Abilene, Town Tamer* and *Law of the Lawless.* His obituary summed it up when it said, "As a Hollywood villain, Mr. MacLane was invariably called upon to portray blustery tough guys, mean outlaws, bullying gangsters and hard-edged convicts."

One of his more memorable roles was in *The Treasure of Sierra Madre,* in which he played a contractor who gave Humphrey Bogart and Tim Holt construction jobs, cheated them out of their wages and then was beaten up by them in a barroom fight. Good movies or bad, MacLane always did a solid job of being a tough guy. And he finally did get his chance at being a good guy, although not in the movies—in 1960, he played a United States marshal who was the hero in a television series called "The Outlaws."

Any connoisseur of tough guys will find it interesting to compare the film style of Barton MacLane with that of another perennial bad guy, Jack Palance. MacLane always played a baddie who had nothing to hide and would deliver his message by punching you in the nose. By contrast, Palance's screen style was to be sneaky bad. "Skulk" is the word that comes to the mind when you see Palance in one of his great screen villain roles.

The tone was set in Palance's first big screen role, as the petty gangster villain in *Panic in the Streets* (a film, incidentally, that was also noteworthy for the excellent work done by Zero Mostel, then only emerging from the ranks of B movies, who played Palance's pudgy, quivering toady).

In the film, Palance has smuggled in a man who has died of the black plague, and Richard Widmark is the doctor who is trying to prevent an epidemic. Palance is utterly convincing as the cheap, vicious crook who can, among other villainies, gun down one old friend in cold blood and throw another, ill with plague, over a bannister in an effort to escape. It is quite fitting that Palance is finally trapped against the rat guards on a ship's hawser.

A high point of Palance's career is his portrayal of the hired gunman who is turned against the decent, honest farmers in the 1953 movie *Shane*. From the moment that he makes his appearance, Palance is a picture of cold, murderous concentration. George Stevens,

PANIC IN THE STREETS
Jack Palance, in hiding, is about to slug Richard Widmark.
The inert body is Zero Mostel.
(*20th Century-Fox, 1950*)

DRACULA

Who else but Bela Lugosi, that matchless vampire?
(*Universal, 1931*)

the director, went to the length of choosing for Palance a horse with a peculiarly mincing, ominous gait.

When Palance taunts a farmer into a duel and then efficiently kills him, you get the distinct impression that this is a man who likes his deadly work; his eyes sparkle with malevolent glee and his lips are drawn back in an unnerving grimace that one hates to call a smile. One measure of Palance's ability to look menacing is the fact that he could play *Dr. Jekyll and Mr. Hyde* on television with almost no make-up. Most actors who have played the role slather on greasepaint for the transformation from the good Dr. Jekyll to the wicked Mr. Hyde. Palance can make the change pretty much on his own.

Occasionally, Palance has played a non-villainous role, but it has always been with heavy undertones of menace. In *Attack!* (1956), one of the most harrowing war movies ever, he was an intense infantry officer dedicated to getting revenge against an incompetent commander; in *The Big Knife,* he played a Hollywood star who was being torn apart by failure. In almost every other one of his appearances, it has been pure evil.

Bela Lugosi offered pure evil of another sort. Lugosi and Boris Karloff were the two great horror-film stars of the 1930s and 1940s, but the images they projected were completely different. Karloff (his real name was William Henry Pratt, and he was born in England) somehow came across as a gentle man. His great horror roles, such as the monster in *Frankenstein* and several sequels, depended rather heavily on good make-up, and his kindly personality managed to come through. One of the reasons why *Frankenstein* is so horrifying is that the audience can sympathize with the great, hulking monster, killer though it may be. That underlying gentleness allowed Karloff to break out of the horror film mold now and then to play straight parts.

Not so with Lugosi. When he appeared in the title role of *Dracula,* the make-up was more or less superfluous, and the evil he radiated appeared to be frighteningly real. Unlike Karloff, Lugosi was never able to break out of the horror business. His straight parts were few and not very successful. In general, he was always the mad scientist, tinkering with nature for his own vile purposes, or a master of some other sort of evil.

You can't blame Hollywood for type-casting Bela Lugosi; he was so good at being bad that there seemed to be no other choice. Just a look down the list of his movie titles can send a shiver down your back: *Murders in the Rue Morgue, White Zombie, The Death Kiss, Island of Lost Souls, The Mark of the Vampire, The Body Snatcher, The Black Sleep.* As the years went on, Lugosi's films tended to get shoddier as horror films first began to get imitative and then lost any originality at all. But even in the worst of the lot, toward the end, Lugosi added a genuine note of horror. Unhappily for his acting pretensions, it appeared, toward the end of his career, that being evil was the only thing he was good at. But he was very good at being very bad. Almost no one else has managed to build a whole career on un-adulterated evil, as Bela Lugosi did.

From Bad
To Good

You all know good-guy Raymond Burr, right? He is the kind, wise, all-seeing attorney, bent on doing justice, in the television series "Perry Mason." He's also the detective in a wheelchair in another TV series, "Ironside," in which he also is justice personified. Good old Raymond Burr.

But how about Raymond Burr, tough guy, cheap punk and sadist? That image might seem highly improbable now, but it happens to be the sort of role that Burr played for the major part of his life on the screen. Born in Canada, Burr broke into the movies as a burly, jowly tough guy, in films with titles like *Raw Deal, Pitfall,* and *Ruthless.* It seemed that he was destined to be the eternal villain. Even when he moved into bigger roles, he was still the bad guy. Notably, he was the killer whom James Stewart stalked through binoculars in the Alfred Hitchcock thriller, *Rear Window,* and he was the hostile district attorney who tormented Montgomery Clift in *A Place in the Sun.* In the mid-1950s, it seemed that Burr was going to be another Barton MacLane, destined to snarl and bully his way through life.

Then along came television, and Perry Mason. It was something of a surprise when Burr got the title role in the series; accustomed to being type-cast, he had gone to audition for the role of the district attorney who lost every case to Perry Mason (William Tallman got that part). Then, for a full ten seasons starting in 1957, Raymond Burr got used to being a hero, and the viewers also got used to seeing him as a good guy. The hero business is better than the villain business for an actor; it was predictable that Burr would stop making films once his nice (but tough) guy image was established on the TV tube. When "Perry Mason" ran out of gas, TV's idea men thought up "Ironside," a neat solution for the job of marketing Burr's new personality. It's safe to say that Raymond Burr is out of the villain market.

Switching from being a bad guy to being a good guy is a smart move, and Raymond Burr is just one of many actors who have managed it. Seldom has the change been so quick and so total (remember, Bogart, Cagney and Robinson went back to gangster parts occasionally all through their lives), but there are many precedents for the shift.

One of those who have made it in more recent years is Clint Eastwood. After a stint on television in the Western series "Rawhide," Eastwood went to Italy to film a series of what are called spaghetti Westerns, in which the dialogue always looks dubbed whether or not it is, and the blood flows like cheap wine. Eastwood played the laconic, hard-bitten "man with no name" in such films as *A Fistful of Dollars, For a Few Dollars More* and *The Good, the Bad and the Ugly.* To everyone's great surprise, these rather offhand films proved to be highly successful at the box office. Eastwood came back to Hollywood to make an American spaghetti Western, *Hang 'Em High,* in which the bullets flew and the bodies fell as freely as they had in Italy.

Then Eastwood became a good guy—although very much a tough one. He was a Western sheriff who came to New York to hunt a killer in *Coogan's Bluff,* and a taciturn cowboy who helped Shirley MacLaine, a shady lady masquerading as a nun, in *Two Mules for Sister Sara.* Later, he played the title role in *Dirty Harry,* a San Francisco cop determined to be at least as brutal as the criminals he is hunting. He came back as Harry a couple of years later in *Magnum Force.* Eastwood is still developing on the screen, but he has changed successfully from a pure villain to an actor who can be the tough sort of good guy that Cagney or Bogart acted so well.

Charles Bronson also has made that transition, and rather improbably. Bronson has always had one strike against him—he just isn't as good looking as a real movie star should be. (His critics say that he has a sec-

A FISTFUL OF DOLLARS
Clint Eastwood, sporting his usual stubble and stogie,
lends a helpful hand.
(*Leone, 1967*)

ond strike. According to them his acting leaves a lot to be desired.) One of fifteen children of a family in the coal-mining region of Pennsylvania, Bronson worked in the mine as a teen-ager. He was drafted during World War II and more or less drifted into acting after discharge. His first Hollywood parts were inconspicuous bits (including a role as what one reviewer called "the most muscular Indian ever to have brandished a rifle before a camera"), but he did get some notice for playing the title role in *Machine Gun Kelly,* a quickie gangster film.

Bronson's parts got somewhat better after that, but he always seemed to be just one of the tough-guy crowd. Almost symbolically, he was one of the seven in *The Magnificent Seven,* a 1960 Western remake of a Japanese samurai saga, and one of the dozen in *The Dirty Dozen,* a 1967 World War II rehash that featured almost unrelieved brutality. Bronson's fortune wasn't made until he went to Europe to make some films. One French movie, *Adieu, l'Ami* (*Farewell, Friend*) was a box-office smash in Europe that never appeared in the United States; another Bronson film, a spaghetti Western called *Once Upon a Time in the West,* certified his appeal as a hard, mean star.

Bronson has been specializing in hero roles that require a liberal dash of almost dehumanized toughness. When he played a detective in a thriller, *Rider on the Rain,* one reviewer summed it up by calling him "wonderfully menacing and tough."

Perhaps his most typical role was the lead in *Death Wish* (1974), a film in which Bronson plays an architect who, after the killing of his wife, starts a personal campaign aimed at ridding New York of muggers. Many people cringed as they watched Bronson methodically gunning down hoods on the screen, but some audiences took the vigilante moral so much to heart that they would break into cheers as Bronson impassively rubbed out another criminal. What mattered to the important people in the film business was that *Death Wish* made a lot of money. Being bad definitely has been good for Charles Bronson, who now can make a secure living being tough and yet legal.

An actor who made an even more complete transition from bad guy to good guy was Lee Marvin, who also starred in *The Dirty Dozen*—not as one of the dozen, but as the colonel who put the crew together. From the beginning of his Hollywood career, Marvin seemed destined to be a perpetual heavy. His thick-lipped, brooding ruggedness were made to order for villainy, and he hardly did a good deed during the early films he made. Filmgoers who appreciate nastiness still recall *The Big Heat,* the 1953 gangster movie in which Marvin is a hoodlum who throws scalding coffee in the face of beautiful Gloria Grahame (and later is killed for his crimes). He was also particularly effective in *Bad Day at Black Rock,* the 1955 movie in which Marvin was one of a gang of hired strong-arm men in a small town who cannot prevent the hero, Spencer Tracy, from uncovering and avenging a long-hidden murder.

But there was more to Lee Marvin than nastiness. He started playing more or less sympathetic film roles,

DEATH WISH

Who could be tougher than Charles Bronson, who is out to
cleanse the city of muggers and hoodlums?
(*Paramount, 1974*)

such as the commanding officer in *Attack!* On television, he was the detective hero of a series called "M Squad" in the 1960s. And the big breakthrough came in the film comedy Western *Cat Ballou* (1965), in which he won the Oscar for a double role as a washed-up hero and a vicious gunman. Ever since then, Lee Marvin's screen personality has been decidedly tough (how could he be anything else with that face?) but also likeable. Why, he could even make a musical, *Paint Your Wagon,* which would have been impossible with the old Lee Marvin of the coffee-throwing days.

You could tell pretty much the same story about another Hollywood tough guy, Anthony Quinn, except that Quinn had to wait longer for success and never seemed to make it as big as Lee Marvin did. The son of an Irish father and a Mexican mother, Quinn spent a very long time playing a wide miscellany of supporting parts in all sorts of movies, many of them nondescript.

If you look fast enough at many of the more forgettable (and a few of the big-time) movies of the 1930s and 1940s, you can spy the young Anthony Quinn in one guise or another. He was a Sioux in Cecil B. DeMille's *The Plainsman,* a Panamanian in *Swing High Swing Low,* a Hawaiian in *Waikiki Wedding,* a Spaniard in *Last Train from Madrid,* an Indian again (Chief Crazy Horse) in *They Died With Their Boots On*—well, you get the idea.

In the 1950s, things began to look up. Quinn won an Oscar for the more-or-less sympathetic (although still thick-skinned) role of the brother in *Viva Zapata* (1952). He managed to portray genuine anguish in a

CAT BALLOU

Lee Marvin played not only the bad guy gunman, shown here,
but also the good guy, in a double role that won him an Oscar.
(*Columbia, 1965*)

great Italian movie, *La Strada* (1956), in which he was a brutish strong man who could still arouse empathy. Rather quietly, Quinn became a star who could attract good roles in A movies. Perhaps his high point was in the title role of *Zorba, the Greek* (1964), as the earthy Greek peasant who taught an intellectual what life and happiness was all about. An even better measure of the way that Quinn's image had grown was the fact that he could play the Pope in *The Shoes of the Fisherman*. The film was ponderous and flopped at the box office, but Anthony Quinn obviously had become something more than just another screen tough guy. He has never really found a top-notch role since then, but it is quite an achievement to have broken out of the Hollywood rut.

You'd have to go back a while and accept a completely different style to find a comparable escape from type casting. No actor could be more unlike Anthony Quinn than Basil Rathbone. While Quinn radiated earthiness, Rathbone was surrounded by an aura of British sophistication, set off by his neatly clipped mustache and his equally neatly clipped accent. While Quinn had to be at home with a bow and arrow, Rathbone was always light-heartedly toying with a cigarette case in modern dramas or with dueling sword in costume epics. The one thing that the two actors had in common during the 1930s was their screen villainy. Skilled with the sword, Rathbone was almost always (at least it seemed that way) being polished off in the last reel by Errol Flynn. If not, he was being villainous in some other way.

Rathbone was the tyrannic second husband, Murdstone, in *David Copperfield* (1935). He was Flynn's sneering French pirate partner and rival in *Captain Blood*. He was the grasping Sir Guy of Gisbourne in *The Adventures of Robin Hood*. He was even Baron Frankenstein in *Son of Frankenstein,* one of the many horror film sequels that Hollywood was turning out in the 1930s.

Rathbone's escape from his career of evil-doing came when his studio asked him to play Sherlock Holmes in the 1939 film version of *The Hound of the Baskervilles.* The same smooth, calculating intelligence that had made Rathbone such a convincing villain allowed him to be an utterly convincing Sherlock Holmes. *The Hound of the Baskervilles* was a success, in part because Rathbone was aided by Nigel Bruce as a suitably dunderheaded Dr. Watson, and the two made a sequel, *The Adventures of Sherlock Holmes,* that was released the same year.

That was only the beginning. Rathbone eventually made a total of fourteen movie appearances as Sherlock Holmes. Most of those films took enormous liberties with the original Arthur Conan Doyle character. In several of the movies, Holmes was moved forward airly in time so that he could help win World War II: The plots were borrowed liberally from the original Sherlock Holmes stories, but mere reality was never allowed to interfere with the fun. The series succeeded because Basil Rathbone was a totally convincing Sherlock Holmes —smooth, rational, quick-witted. Indeed, to a whole generation, Basil Rathbone *was* Sherlock Holmes. Other

THE HOUND OF THE BASKERVILLES

Basil Rathbone as Sherlock Holmes and Nigel Bruce
as Dr. Watson. The role rescued Rathbone
from an uninterrupted career as a villain.
(*20th Century-Fox, 1939*)

actors may portray Holmes with equal success, but none
of them will be better at capturing the spirit of the great
detective.

There's a closing chapter to the Rathbone story. After
his long run as Holmes, Rathbone escaped from the
character to return to villainy in films including Danny
Kaye's comedy, *The Court Jester* (1956), as well as
more serious efforts such as *The Mad Doctor* and *The
Comedy of Terrors*. It was a case of once a villain always
a villain.

As a contrast to Rathbone, one can study the career
of Vincent Price, who went in the opposite direction—
from good guy to horrific bad guy. Price has had a
long acting career, first on the stage and later in the
movies, but his real financial success came only when
he went into horror movies, playing deep-eyed villains
with a tongue-in-cheek, wink-at-the-audience approach.

If you're a fan of old movies, you may have picked
out Vincent Price in such roles as the bewigged King
Charles II of *Hudson's Bay* and the doomed Duke of
Clarence of *The Tower of London* (killed, incidentally,
by order of Basil Rathbone, playing King Richard III).
Price gradually edged over into roles of villainy—or, at
least, wishy-washiness—including the weak-kneed suitor
in the thriller *Laura,* the wicked Boss Tweed of a
Deanna Durbin musical, *Up in Central Park,* and the
silly soap tycoon in a Ronald Colman comedy of 1950,
Champagne for Caesar. Then came horror, and real success.

It started with *House of Wax,* the 1953 film in
which Price played the hideously scarred owner of a
wax museum whose effigies contain real bodies. It was

a time when Hollywood was trying almost anything it could think of to fight television, and the movie was made in 3-D (the audience wore special glasses to get the three-dimensional effect).

Price made a few non-horror films, picked up the horror theme in a 1958 movie, *The Fly,* in which a scientist's experiments cause a terrible mutation, and then really hit his stride with a long series of low-budget films based on the stories of Edgar Allan Poe: *The House of Usher* (1960), *The Pit and the Pendulum* (1961), *Tales of Terror* (1962), *The Raven* (1963), *The Masque of the Red Death* (1964). Price has the kind of mad laugh, plummy voice and wild-eyed flamboyance that makes you realize that what you see on the screen, however terrifying, is really just in fun— well, maybe.

His later titles even made fun of the horror theme; what else could a title such as *The Abominable Dr. Phibes* be telling you? Anyway, films of that kind kept the money pouring in and enabled Price to enjoy his art collection, which he has added to regularly. The audiences who pay to see Vincent Price grimace and giggle though all those horror films are, in a peculiar way, making a contribution to culture, believe it or not. You can check it out with the appropriate art dealer.

Once in a While

Tough guys don't have to be bad guys all the time. In fact, there are quite a few instances of screen stars who have played tough, bad guys only once or twice, and then have moved on to other things. Take Paul Muni, for instance.

He seemed destined for a long string of tough-guy roles when he made *Scarface*, the 1932 film that was based on the story of Al Capone. With a scar streaking down his left cheek and his eyes glinting, Muni made quite an impression as the young punk with a quick gun who shoots his way to the top of the gang world before dying a cowardly death. (As a sidelight, *Scarface* had Boris Karloff playing a Chicago gangster with an incongruous English accent.) But instead of going on to play more gangsters on the screen, Muni quickly established himself as a dignified leading man who was most at home in the kind of righteous film biographies that Hollywood made in great number during the 1930s.

True, Muni's next film after *Scarface* had him playing a convict. But the film, *I Am a Fugitive From a Chain Gang,* was an exposé of the degrading conditions in Southern prisons of the time. Muni played a man who is somewhat unjustly sentenced to prison and who endures the full range of cruelties found in the Southern penal system—shackles, whippings, beatings, poor food, and more. Muni escapes in the end, but the film has nothing like a happy ending. In a final scene that is one of the most striking ever made, he has a few hasty words on a dark street with the woman he loves. When he starts to leave, she asks desperately, "Will you write? How do you live?" As Muni fades into the shadows, he hisses hopelessly, "I steal."

With his star status established, Muni was able to choose his scripts with care. He showed a social conscience by playing a coal miner fighting for the rights of working men in *Black Fury* (1935). After that came a string of film biographies: *The Story of Louis Pasteur, The Life of Emile Zola,* and *Juarez,* all of which were greeted enthusiastically. Muni got an Oscar for his portrayal of Zola. It was a long way from *Scarface.*

Unfortunately, Muni's screen success faded rapidly. In later years, he made relatively few films. Today, critics find that his film acting lacks subtlety and is too melodramatic. Nevertheless, Muni did show that a determined actor could escape from the tough-guy type casting of the Hollywood system.

SCARFACE

Paul Muni made his movie reputation with this gangster
film, but he hardly ever played a bad guy again.
(*United Artists, 1932*)

A more limited actor who made the same escape, but not quite as well, was Alan Ladd. Like Muni, Ladd's first big screen appearance was as a killer. In *This Gun for Hire,* released in 1942, Ladd was quietly impressive as the laconic but deadly hired gunman named Raven. His most impressive characteristic was his ability to radiate a cold deadliness. His weakness was his monotonous voice and rigid acting.

But in the films that followed, often playing alongside Veronica Lake, Ladd was impressively tough. (It helped that Veronica Lake's acting ability was not going to throw anyone else into the shadows; her success at that time was built to a great extent on her gimmicky hairdo, with tresses flowing over one eye— sort of an early version of Farrah Fawcett-Majors.)

After the first bad-guy role in *This Gun for Hire,* Ladd rarely played a villain. He was definitely the tough guy though. In films such as *The Glass Key* and *The Blue Dahlia* he was a vulnerable tough guy, who was basically innocent but had to fight hard to prove it. *The Blue Dahlia,* for example, featured Ladd as a war veteran who returned to a faithless wife, and who was accused of her murder. Tight-lipped, Ladd found the real killer (of course), but his very tight-lippedness made the way harder.

Ladd's best single part was in the title role of *Shane.* Again he was the tough guy who was somehow innocent—in this Western, a gunman who had given up his trade and went back to the gun reluctantly to help the farmers who had befriended him. In *Shane,* Alan Ladd somehow gives the impression of never speaking a word.

His past history is never really explained; it is assumed from his attitude. When he buckles on his holster and goes off for the inevitable showdown with the hired killer, Jack Palance, it is without a word of explanation. The movie ends with Shane riding off into the prairie, presumably to his death from the gunshot wounds he has suffered, as silently as he arrived. After *Shane,* Ladd made a series of largely mediocre movies, with such titles as *Saskatchewan, Drum Beat,* and *Guns of the Timberland,* before his premature death.

The character who turned out to be the murderer in *The Blue Dahlia* was Ladd's side-kick, played by William Bendix. In that film, Bendix was rather a victim of circumstances, someone who had been thrown out of whack by a head wound suffered in World War II. That role was something of a departure for Bendix, a Brooklyn-born lad of burly build and irregular features who started acting at the age of 5, played minor league baseball briefly, and then drifted into the movies, where he specialized in playing the typical Brooklyn type of the era.

Those were the days of war dramas that usually had a representative spectrum of Americans—one guy named Tex, another named Nebraska, and so on. Bendix played the guy who was nicknamed Tex. He was not too bright, ready with his fists, and said "dese" and "dose" a lot.

But the William Bendix character also had a dark side that was displayed only rarely. *The Blue Dahlia* showed that side. A movie called *The Dark Corner* showed it even better. In *The Dark Corner,* Bendix was a rumpled, ruthless killer who was hired to make life difficult for the good guy, who was played by Mark Stevens. (One sidelight of the film is the fact that the heroine was played by Lucille Ball, who was then struggling through a long series of serious roles in the years before it was discovered that she had a talent for comedy.) Bendix came to a sticky end; he was shoved out the window of a skyscraper by the man who had hired him, and who was expressing dissatisfaction with the job done by the hired gun.

It was somehow improbable to see good old William Bendix as a brutal gunman. He hardly ever repeated that sort of role. He was much more familiar in the television series "The Life of Riley," a sort of forerunner of "All in the Family" with Bendix as the bedeviled father, which ran for most of the 1950s. But if you think Bendix as a gunman was odd, consider the man who shoved him out the window in *The Dark Corner.* That was Clifton Webb, who came into movies as a dancer and who is best remembered as the waspish, supercultivated baby sitter in *Sitting Pretty* and the rest of the Mr. Belvedere series.

Clifton Webb's screen character was always pretty nasty, but it was generally a high-society sort of nastiness, expressed mainly by looking down at those who do not recognize the correct cut of a gentleman's suit or the theme from a Beethoven piano sonata. *The Dark Corner* was one movie in which Webb's nastiness became murderous.

A much more memorable thriller in which he was the heavy was *Laura,* a 1944 detective story that gave the world a memorable title tune. Webb played a theater critic named Waldo Lydecker in *Laura* (he had played the owner of an art gallery in *The Dark Corner;* Webb may have been an occasional murderer, but he was definitely a refined murderer), and he gave the distinct impression of being able to kill someone who was not up to his standards of good taste.

It was somewhat unfortunate that an actor with such an ability to portray sheer nastiness should have been steered into more respectable parts, but Hollywood wanted it that way. As Mr. Belvedere, Webb was supposed to be highly educated, condescending and lovable in spite of himself. Audiences bought the act. They even bought Webb as a hero—although a hero with an acid, demanding personality: John Philip Sousa, the march king, in the biography *Stars and Stripes Forever,* and even as an Allied officer who came up with a grisly scheme to outwit the Nazis in *The Man Who Never Was.* (The scheme: obtain the right kind of corpse and have it wash ashore in Nazi-occupied Europe with papers that would mislead the Germans about the time and place of the upcoming invasion of Europe. Supposedly, it really happened.)

If you can't believe Clifton Webb as a naval officer, would you believe Walter Matthau as a whip-cracking backwoods villain? Probably not, but that was how it was in a film called *The Kentuckian,* which introduced Matthau to the screen in 1955. The star of the film was Burt Lancaster, and one of the highlights was a whip fight between noble Lancaster and villainous Matthau. "I did it because I was desperately short of money," Walter Matthau explained later. He did a lot of things for money in his early film years, playing a series of forgettable bad-guy roles, most of them very, very distant from his upbringing on the sidewalks of New York; another Western villain in a Kirk Douglas movie, *The Indian Fighter,* a bad guy in an Elvis Presley film, *King Creole,* a drunken judge in an Audie Murphy Western, *Ride a Crooked Trail.*

All the time, Matthau's talent was there, waiting to be discovered. He made the transition to leading parts slowly, edging over by starting to play roles that were villainous, but at least comically villainous—for example, a supposed Greek gangster in a Robert Preston movie, *Island of Love.* What really helped Matthau was winning awards on the Broadway stage, in plays that he took time off to do when he wasn't working hard in Hollywood to meet his alimony payments and support his gambling habit. After that, Matthau began getting the good parts he deserved.

He was the original Oscar Madison, the sloppy half of *The Odd Couple,* which first was a play, then a movie and then a successful television series. He was the unscrupulous "Whiplash Willie" Gingrich, a shyster lawyer who manipulated his brother-in-law, played by Jack Lemmon, into getting a big insurance settlement, in Billy Wilder's black comedy, *The Fortune Cookie.* He was a man-of-the-world dentist in *Cactus Flower,* a comedy in which Ingrid Bergman got Matthau in the end.

The old toughness is still there, but it's a comic toughness now. As the detective solving a strange mass killing in *The Laughing Policeman,* as the hard-as-nails

THE FRONT PAGE
Walter Matthau as the tough-talking managing editor, in
Hollywood's latest version of the newspaper story.
(*Universal, 1974*)

managing editor in the latest remake of that old newspaper saga, *The Front Page* (again teamed with Jack Lemmon), as the police lieutenant in *The Taking of Pelham One Two Three,* Matthau has been a tough guy who uses wisecracks as his primary weapon. If Walter Matthau makes any Westerns in the future, one can picture him firing off punch lines, not shotguns—certainly never wielding a whip as he once did.

You'd also have to look far back to find a villainous tough-guy role by George C. Scott, who now is being acclaimed as one of the best actors around. And Scott has never been a whip-swinger. His villainy is quiet, cultivated and calculated.

You can see it in *The Hustler,* a film in which Paul Newman played a callow young pool player, out to challenge the steady old pro, Minnesota Fats, who was played by Jackie Gleason. In *The Hustler,* George C. Scott is the head man who coolly looks over the young contender and dismisses him as a punk—an evaluation that is proven correct when Newman cracks under the strain. Scott was a more comic villain, although a chilling one, in *Dr. Strangelove,* a movie that manages to be funny about the grimmest subject of all, nuclear war. Scott makes his character, a Red-hating, sky-happy Air Force general, seem loonily real as the picture careens along a road to nuclear destruction.

What everyone remembers Scott for is his portrayal in *Patton,* the biography of the World War II general who lived only for combat. Scott won an Oscar (which he refused to accept) for his portrait of a man who believed that war was the highest peak of the human race, who believed in reincarnation, who could lead an army better than he could control his tongue.

It took a great actor to make this mass of contradictions believable, and Scott did it almost perfectly. Unfortunately, most of his other movies have not been up to his level. In *The Flim Flam Man,* a comedy about a rural con artist, he was miscast in a role that would have been better suited for W. C. Fields. In *The Last Run,* he managed to bring some depth to the part of a retired driver of getaway cars who was doing one last job for the mob.

One exception to the mediocrity of his roles was *The Hospital,* written by Paddy Chayevsky, in which Scott played a doctor who had been burned out by his personal and professional troubles, and who could coldly and professionally set about committing suicide in the most efficient and painless way possible. The inner toughness of the man comes out when he refuses to go away with the woman he loves because that would mean abandoning his responsibility to the beleaguered slum hospital where he works. The story sounds grim in outline, and grimmer if one mentions the two or three murders that occur along the way, but it is cruelly funny in the way that Chayevsky's later attack on television, "Network," is funny: You laugh because the truth is painfully comic.

In a way, George C. Scott's story was a replay of an earlier Hollywood saga, that of Spencer Tracy. Like Scott, Tracy hardly ever played a villainous role; his part as a hardened criminal in one of the first big prison movies, *20,000 Years in Sing Sing* (1933), was a rare exception. Later in the 1930s, Tracy played a string of good guys, winning an Oscar as the Portuguese fisherman in *Captains Courageous* (1937).

Often, Tracy showed up on screen as a Catholic priest—as Father Flanagan in *Boys Town,* and an inevitable sequel, *Men of Boys Town,* and as the clerical friend of Clark Gable, the gambler, in *San Francisco,* for example. In the 1940s, he made a number of memorable films with Katharine Hepburn, with whom he had a long relationship.

Toughness, but a quiet kind of toughness, was Spencer Tracy's specialty. His sort of toughness showed up very well alongside the wit and cultivation of Hepburn. Their first film, *Woman of the Year* (1942), set the pattern. Tracy played a newspaper sports writer, Hepburn a political columnist who is at home in all languages and with all the great leaders of the world. They meet, argue and marry, in the accepted style of the romantic comedies of that era. Then come the arguments—her career against his, her priorities against his. He wants to walk out on her; she wants to walk out on him. In his tough but quiet way, he finally explains that they can love each other without changing very much: happy ending.

There was another happy ending in *Pat and Mike,* a film in which Hepburn is an all-star woman athlete and Tracy is the Brooklyn-type sports manager who takes her under his wing. One of the choice lines in the film comes when Tracy casts an eye at his athlete during a workout and tells a friend: "There ain't much meat there, but what there is, is cherce."

BAD DAY AT BLACK ROCK

Even though he's wearing a black hat, Spencer Tracy is the
good guy who turns out to be tougher than bad guy Robert Ryan.
(*MGM, 1955*)

The special kind of Spencer Tracy toughness showed up best in *Bad Day at Black Rock,* one of his later films. He plays a quiet, one-armed man who steps off the train in a tiny, sun-baked desert town one day after World War II is over and asks for an old Japanese resident. Quickly, things get very tense and very rough. Tracy is taunted by bully boys, denied answers, ridden off the road when he goes for a drive, and provoked into a fight with one of the town's brawlers, Ernest Borgnine. Tracy wins the fight with a few slashing karate chops that leave Borgnine bloody and gasping for air in the dust. Tracy goes on from there to solve the mystery and bring the wrongdoers to justice, in his contained, unpretentious way.

In a way, *Bad Day at Black Rock,* made in 1955, was one of the last movies of a vanishing era—the era when it was easy to tell the good guys from the bad guys, when the hero always married the heroine, and when there wasn't all that much variety to movie plots. Mass production of films has ended today, as television has taken over that end of the market. Mass employment of actors by Hollywood has also ended, as the "stock companies" once maintained by the big studios have been disbanded. A look back at some of the faces in the crowd will show just what we're missing these days.

The Old Reliables

Hollywood in its glory days needed a steady supply of bad guys to complete the roughly symmetrical triangles that were the center of most of its plots. Quite often the triangle was good guy-bad guy-girl. The good guy got the girl and the bad guy got his comeuppance. Alternatively, the triangle could be hero-villain-money. The hero won the money (or the gold mine or the railroad or the throne or whatever) and the villain got the wrong end of a sword or the equivalent. The plot could be varied somewhat by pulling the old switcheroo—that is, by making the villain the hero.

In films such as *Public Enemy* and *Little Caesar,* the movie makers walked a fine line, loudly proclaiming the dreadfulness of the way their gangster got ahead but nevertheless making villainy seem almost attractive. Everything was put right when all wrongdoing was suitably punished at the conclusion; punishment for wrongdoing was a basic requirement of the code that governed movies in those days.

Since there were ample employment opportunities for sneerers, skulkers, scoundrels and various other no-goods, the law of supply and demand operated to fill the need. A cheerful thought for the actors who stepped forth manfully to give the audience someone to hiss was that there was usually room for advancement. As we have already seen from the progress of the great Hollywood tough guys, a lifetime of pure villainy was rare. In the early nickelodeon days, when films were silent and short and audiences were unsophisticated, villainy had to be black-hearted and unreformable. But as the movies grew up, both audiences and directors began to see greater possibilities in the characters of the bad guys.

Perhaps the best example of the changing ways of movie menace was the career of one of the more outstanding middle-rank Hollywood tough guys, Wallace Beery. The story has a prologue, because Wallace Beery himself was the brother of an actor who was hardly ever anything but a bad guy. Starting with the silent films, the brother, Noah Beery, grimaced and threatened his way through a villainous career that ran into the 1940s. Never really a star, Noah Beery was always available to be a heavy in a Grade-B Western or in one of the penny-dreadful serials that Hollywood ground out endlessly in the era when movies were king.

Wallace Beery also began acting in the silents, but in an unexpected way—in skirts, playing the ludicrous role of a grotesque Swedish housemaid in one-reel comedies. After he got out of skirts, Beery moved on to a long series of film roles as an oafish villain. However, after a while it became apparent that Beery was a villain with comic possibilities. His rugged features seemed to be on the verge of a bashful smile even during the most threatening moments. And when sound arrived, Beery's peculiar bass voice, which had a marvelous resemblance to the croaking of a frog, made him seem even more sympathetic.

Wallace Beery could slouch on the screen with one hand holding a bag of money from a bank robbery and the other holding a smoking six-shooter, but when he rumpled his hair, growled, "Aw, shucks," and went into a twisted little smile, the audience had the feeling that he would never pull the trigger on an honest man, and that he probably had a good reason for stealing the money in the first place. The rule was relentless: as a villain, Beery had to pay the price of his crime. But in films such as *The Bad Man of Brimstone,* there was always a sentimental reason for the crime and time for a tearful scene before Beery headed for prison or a rope.

In the 1930s, with the help of some shrewd casting, Beery parlayed his mannerisms into stardom. He was always the tough guy with a heart of gold. Even in the role of Long John Silver in *Treasure Island* (1934), Beery managed to give a sentimental tinge to as hard-hearted a villain as has ever been sketched.

TREASURE ISLAND
Wallace Beery is trying out his somewhat battered charm
on child star Jackie Cooper.
(*Paramount, 1934*)

Sentiment stood Beery in good stead as his importance began to decline. In the 1940s, he made a series of financially successful minor Westerns with such titles as *Twenty-Mule Team* and *Jackass Mail.* His co-star was Marjorie Main, whose weathered appearance and gravel voice were perfectly suited to playing alongside Beery. The later Wallace Beery movies show up now and then on television. They are pure corn, but the corn is from an era that had achieved a high degree of expertise at producing it, and the films are still fun to watch.

No actor could be more unlike Wallace Beery in appearance than Peter Lorre, but the careers of the two ran parallel to a remarkable degree. That wasn't surprising, given the needs of the Hollywood studios. They were turning out movies just about as fast as the cameras could roll, and there wasn't much time for subtle casting in those frantic mass-production days. Once a label was slapped on an actor it stayed on, and only the most strenuous efforts could change the label.

Peter Lorre sidled onto the Hollywood scene in the 1930s well labeled as a crawly continental bad guy, and that is largely what he remained for many years. Before he came to Hollywood, Lorre had shown considerable acting depth in a number of European films. Perhaps his most striking role was in a German movie, starkly titled *M,* directed in 1931 by the great Fritz Lang.

In this film, Lorre plays a child killer who so terrorizes a city that the criminals band together to capture and try him after the police fail. Even today, despite scratchy prints, primitive screen techniques, and unsatisfactory subtitles, *M* can still terrorize an audience. It's interesting to note that the original film, old as it is, gets shown more in revival houses than the 1950 American remake of the same title, even though David Wayne did a commendable job in the title role. The scene in which the cringing Lorre screams out his anguish at the forces within him that drive him to kill is unforgettable.

Hollywood was interested in Lorre mostly because of his bulgy-eyed appearance and odd accent. Lorre was a Hungarian, but the accent could be twisted into any nationality that suited the producer. Perhaps the oddest use of it, and of Lorre, came when he made eight films as Mr. Moto, a Japanese detective who was popular in the 1930s. The series came to an abrupt end after Pearl Harbor, when Lorre began playing wartime roles.

He was a useful, all-around villain, occasionally a hero, from almost any country you could name: A Chinese ship's captain in a Clark Gable adventure, *They Met in Bombay;* a Nazi spy in *All Through the Night;* rather indefinable in two of his best roles, Joel Cairo in *The Maltese Falcon* and Ugatti in *Casablanca,* both with Bogart and Sydney Greenstreet; a Russian agent in *Background to Danger;* a French sergeant in *Cross of Lorraine;* a Spanish conspirator in *Confidential Agent;* and so on and on and on.

Lorre always did a good job and usually much more in parts that too often were beneath his skills. Unhappily, Hollywood never appreciated his talents justly, and he slipped into a decline. In the 1950s and 1960s he got mostly Grade-B movies or minor parts, often parodying the Peter Lorre who had become a standard part of the act of any night-club impersonator. Maybe the best of the lot was an outrageous spoof called *Beat the Devil;* you can get the tone of the film when you hear that Lorre played a Chilean of German descent whose name was O'Hara. After that, it was mostly mugging it up in Jerry Lewis movies or in horror cheapies like *Tales of Terror*—an unhappy end for an actor with Lorre's skills.

Any time you think of Peter Lorre you have to think of Sydney Greenstreet. They played together a dozen times or so and made an ideal pairing. Greenstreet was just as versatile as Lorre. Just as Lorre's Hungarian accent could suggest any number of possible backgrounds, Greenstreet's rumbling British accent allowed him to slide easily from role to role: an American Civil War general, Winfield Scott, in *They Died With Their Boots On;* an Arab entrepreneur in *Casablanca;* a pro-German Frenchman in *Passage to Marseilles;* an Italian archvillain in *The Woman in White,* a florid film version of one of the great detective stories of the nineteenth century.

When Lorre and Greenstreet got together in a film, the odds were high that these two old pros would steal the picture from your standard Hollywood leading man. It took someone with the screen personality of Bogart to keep Greenstreet and Lorre from taking over.

The surprising thing about Sydney Greenstreet's film career was that he had one at all. He was sixty years old and had been on the stage in the United States for nearly four decades when John Huston asked Greenstreet to play the role of Guttman in *The Maltese Falcon.* That first screen role was so well received that Warner Brothers signed him to a long-term contract. Most of his films after that included either Bogart or Lorre or both.

One of their best thrillers was *Three Strangers,* an out-of-the-fog suspense drama that starred Greenstreet as an unscrupulous British barrister who is desperate for money, Lorre as a cockney petty criminal and Geraldine Fitzgerald as the woman who brings them together for a supernatural partnership involving a lottery ticket and a Chinese idol. It would be unfair to give away the plot; let's just say that if this one shows up on television, try to stick with it until the very end.

All in all, Greenstreet spent not much more than ten years making films. He worked hard, though, at one time appearing in twenty-four movies in just eight years. One mark of the success that both Greenstreet and Lorre achieved is the durability of the images they created. Greenstreet's last film was made more than twenty years ago, Lorre's more than a decade ago. Yet the characteristics of the menacing fat man and the sly little man are still familiar to most of us.

You could say the same thing about a Hollywood reliable of a very different sort, George Raft. It isn't that Raft created a lasting impression as an actor; by common agreement, he was never a very good actor at all. But any time a film maker wants to give a quick impression of a cheap gangster, it can be done by using the old image of George Raft that remains in the public mind: the nattily dressed yet somehow greasy mob figure who stands with impassive face and flips a coin over and over. Raft actually did play exactly that character, but for comic effect only, as Spats Colombo in *Some Like It Hot* (1959). By then, Raft was pretty much a Hollywood has-been, and a lot of critics were asking why an actor with such limited ability had been able to have such a long run in the movies.

The answer seems to be that George Raft played so many gangsters on film because of an abiding suspicion that it might have been his real-life role. The question of Raft's ties to the underworld has often been raised. No matter what the answer might be, the aura of underworld connections that hung around him seemed to entrance producers.

It's almost forgotten now that George Raft did some dancing in some early films, such as *Bolero* (1934) and *Rumba* (1935), and that his success in a long string of gangland films such as *Each Dawn I Die* and *Invisible Stripes* actually made him the first choice for the starring roles in *Casablanca, The Maltese Falcon* and *High Sierra*.

In each case, Raft turned down the role and the film makers had to settle for Humphrey Bogart. If you want to exercise your imagination, try to picture any of those three films with George Raft instead of Bogart playing the lead. The daydreams of a whole generation of young people might be completely different.

If you want to be unkind, you can say that the best thing George Raft ever did on screen was not to appear in *Casablanca* and *The Maltese Falcon*. But even if you say that, you have to be impressed with the im-

INVISIBLE STRIPES

The title refers to ex-cons, and George Raft got equal
billing with Humphrey Bogart in this film.
(*Warner Brothers, 1940*)

pact George Raft had on Hollywood. After all, he got a tribute that has been given to very few Hollywood stars: his film biography, *The George Raft Story,* was made while he was still alive. And Raft has achieved screen immortality of a sort; any time a hoodlum starts flipping a coin in a gangster film, the spirit of George Raft is there.

With that one gesture, George Raft may have achieved more memorability than an actor who seemed to be far above him in ability at the time, John Garfield. One of the big young movie stars of the 1930s and 1940s, Garfield died tragically young, while his career had run into trouble, during the Hollywood witch-hunting days of the 1950s. This tough young kid from the streets of New York was accused of having sympathy with communism, and that was enough to ruin a career in that era.

Garfield made his debut as a cynical young musician in a warm-hearted family saga of 1938 called *Four Daughters.* The movie did well enough to spawn a sequel, *Daughters Courageous.* By then, Garfield's screen personality was established. He was the cocky little kid from the wrong side of the street, with plenty of brains and able to use his fists if he had to, always fighting the world to get the good things that came so easily to others and so hard to him. Sometimes he could be a hero, as in the wartime movies *Destination Tokyo* and *Pride of the Marines,* but more often than not he was a crook—a man on the run in *They Made Me a Criminal,* a convict in *Castle on the Hudson* (the "castle" was Sing Sing), a murderer in *The Postman Always*

Rings Twice, a smooth gangland operator in *Force of Evil.*

Maybe the best movie Garfield made was *Body and Soul,* a 1947 film in which he played a young boxer from the Lower East Side of New York. As you might have expected from the films of those days, Garfield's screen mother wanted him to go into something more genteel than boxing, but he went into the ring because there was no other way to make money in the Depression years.

Naturally the mob moves in as Garfield battles his way to the championship, and naturally there is a showdown in which he is ordered to dump a title fight. One of the great fight scenes of any movie was shot for *Body and Soul* by cameraman James Wong Howe, who maneuvered his camera fluidly to show the last exciting minutes when Garfield wins both the fight and his honesty back. Garfield never lost that honesty, until death cut his career short.

When Garfield broke into the movies in *Four Daughters,* the quiet little man with the quizzical smile who played the father of the family was Claude Rains, an English-born actor who was to have his share of bad-guy roles on the screen. To look at him in *Four Daughters,* you wouldn't have thought that Claude Rains had a bad bone in his body; he was a man of obvious cultivation and good humor who wouldn't hurt anyone. But Rains was an actor whose range was broad enough to encompass evil as well as good. Any time Hollywood needed a bad guy who could radiate sophistication and continental smoothness, Rains was a good choice.

Claude Rains had one of the most unusual screen debuts on record, in the title role of the 1933 thriller, *The Invisible Man.* He played a scientist who has made an elixir that gives the power of invisibility and has tried it on himself. The scene where Rains unwraps his bandaged head to disclose only a space where the head should be is unforgettable. Later, he was the once-honest but now corrupt Senator Payne in *Mr. Smith Goes to Washington,* the smilingly corrupt (but ultimately anti-Nazi) French police chief in *Casablanca,* and a Nazi spy who fell in love with an American counterspy, Ingrid Bergman, in Alfred Hitchcock's *Notorious.*

Rains made *Notorious* in 1946, at the end of the boom time for war villains in Hollywood. Anyone with the capacity to sneer, something resembling a German accent and the ability to hold a monocle in his eye could make a good living on the screen during World War II. The irony of the situation was that many of the actors who appeared in Nazi roles on the screen were dedicated anti-Nazis; several of them were European actors who had been driven from their homeland by the real Nazis.

For example, Conrad Veidt was a highly respected actor who had a long and distinguished career in Germany and who left when Hitler took power. Veidt's work in Hollywood gave only a hint of his real ability as an actor. Typically, he was the wicked vizer in *The Thief of Baghdad,* a 1940 fantasy that was most notable for its special effects. When war came, Veidt played almost nothing but Nazis. He was Colonel

Strasser in *Casablanca,* and played a series of stereo-typed roles in such films as *Whistling in the Dark* and *Nazi Agent.*

It was rather unfortunate that the real horror of Nazi rule could not be captured by the wartime films made in Hollywood. Perhaps that was inevitable. American movies were not equipped to deal with the cold-blooded mass murder that was the official policy of the Third Reich. Instead, the films offered cardboard characters—Nazis who sneered and strutted and killed, but who could always be overcome by the clever underground workers in occupied Europe or by the clean young Americans.

As was mentioned earlier, Erich von Stroheim made an ideal Nazi for films. So did Otto Preminger, who had just the right nasty accent, shaved head and bull neck. A villain who was only slightly less believable was Raymond Massey, a Canadian-born actor who was capable of playing heroes (for example, the title role in *Abe Lincoln in Illinois*) but specialized more in smiling yet deadly bad guys. No one could strut across the screen in the medal-heavy black uniform of a Nazi officer with more arrogance than Raymond Massey.

Austrian-born Walter Slezak was more the oily type of Nazi, less arrogant, sneakier but no less treacherous than Massey. In *Lifeboat,* an Alfred Hitchcock movie about survivors of a torpedoed ship, Slezak played the rescued U-boat captain who could be overcome only when all the other passengers united against him.

The wartime portrayal of Japanese on the American screen was a rather shameful affair. Those were the years when many thousands of completely innocent Japanese of American descent were interned out of fears that they might all be spies—something that was never even mentioned in connection with Americans of German and Italian descent. The same naïve racism came across on the screen. Japanese were invariably torture-minded, treacherous and cruel; the irony was that the movie Japanese were often played by Chinese actors.

Some sense of perspective returned when the war was over. In *Notorious,* the German spy played by Claude Rains was certainly evil and destined for no good end, but he was also genuinely fond of his mother and really in love with Ingrid Bergman. In *The Bridge on the River Kwai,* Sessue Hayakawa was a Japanese commanding officer who was cruel enough to drive many of his prisoners to death by overwork. But he was also a man with a clearly defined code of honor and with feelings, a human being who could feel his humiliation at the hands of the British officers who were his prisoners.

Looking back, it's hard to realize just how many actors had a shot at being villains during World War II. Good old Leo G. Carroll, a British import who specialized in suave roles, was a master spy in a 1945 film, *The House on Ninety-Second Street.* Carroll was to return to the spy business in postwar years, often on the good-guy side of the fence, as in the Cary Grant movie *North by Northwest* and the television series "The Man from UNCLE." It is rather odd that one of his least distinguished pieces of work, as a bemused Cosmo

Topper in a second-rate television series, "Topper," should come back to the television screen more often than his better parts.

George Sanders, who played more than his share of bad guys in more than thirty years on the screen, stepped forward to be a Nazi in World War II. He was the suave but ruthless German officer in such films as *Confessions of a Nazi Spy* and *Man Hunt* before he got back to his peacetime screen occupation, which mostly consisted of being a languid rotter, with a casual British drawl and an appealing way of taking property that was not his own. From time to time, Sanders would don armor to do his villainy (he was killed in a clanging screen duel by Robert Taylor in *Ivanhoe*) but his real skill was in modern waspishness; he got an Oscar for playing a sharp-tongued critic in *All About Eve*, a 1950 film in which Hollywood played homage to the legitimate theater.

Even Lee J. Cobb had a whack at playing a Nazi in a 1942 film, *Paris Calling*. Cobb (who was born Leo Jacob in New York) spent most of the war playing burly heroes, in parts that never were worthy of his acting ability. As was often the case, he had to go to Broadway for a success that won him better screen roles. After Cobb created the role of the doomed Willy Loman in one of the great plays of the era, *Death of a Salesman*, he was allowed to be a screen tough guy on a large scale.

Cobb was memorable as the gang leader determined to crush a defiant Marlon Brando in *On the Waterfront*. He was just as good as the snarling, lip-curling juror in *12 Angry Men,* one of the most unusual and moving court dramas ever filmed (it takes place entirely in the jury room, as the fate of a boy accused of murder is argued out). He was properly gross and vulgar as the crude father in *The Brothers Karamazov,* a flawed screen version of the Dostoevsky novel. Later, his Nazi days well behind him, Cobb settled down to a series of tough cop roles, in films like *Our Man Flint* and *Coogan's Bluff.*

But after you list all the famous names who played wartime villains, some tribute must be paid to the almost anonymous army of actors who were recruited to fill the ranks of the henchmen. Being a henchman was, at that time, a well-established if not spectacular way to making a living in Hollywood.

Over several decades, the major and minor studios had been turning out undistinguished gangland and Western films. In the gangland films, there was always a need for someone to be beaten up by the hero, to be shot down almost incidentally when the plot called for some appropriate bloodshed, to sit around a cheap furnished room and play endless games of poker in the background while the star did his business in the foreground. In the Westerns a large supply of warm bodies was needed to rustle cattle, lose bar-room brawls, fall off cliffs when the bad men were cornered by the good guys and shot it out, and to insult respectable women so that the hero could establish his good-guy credentials.

In the Westerns that were ground out relentlessly by such as Tom Mix, Gene Autry and William Boyd (as Hopalong Cassidy), there were two basic types of villains. First there was your ordinary working-hand villain, whose reasons for entering that line of work seemed rather obscure. It was true that being a member of a holdup gang in the Old West was good, clean work that kept a man in the fresh air a lot. But the opportunities for recreation were rather limited and the mortality rate from lead poisoning was distressingly high. In addition, the gang member usually had to cultivate a thin mustache and wear only black hats, so that the audience could tell who to hiss during the fights.

Your second kind of villain was the respectable banker, who wore a vest and a gold watch, smiled pleasantly at the right moments but could not be trusted because he (a) was out to get the ranch away from the heroine by fair means or foul, or (b) was the secret leader of the gang that had been holding up stagecoaches and running cattle off ranches at night, pausing only to burn down a house or two.

It hardly does any good to call off the names of those many actors who did faithful duty as bad guys in Grade-B films. Those Westerns and gangland movies exist somewhere now, but they are rarely shown and would have a modern-day audience either yawning or laughing in minutes. What do such names as Charles King, Fred Kohler, LeRoy Mason and Roy Bancroft mean these days, despite all their hours of screen villainy?

In the early days of television, it seemed that a new generation would have a chance to appreciate the sound professionalism of screen villains when the Hopalong Cassidy films had their hour of popularity on television. But the hour soon passed, and TV audiences became too sophisticated to allow any further revivals of the standard Western that once was an accepted item as the bottom part of a double feature. Indeed, even the double feature has faded away. Film audiences today seem to prefer one bloated three-hour film to the two taut ninety-minute features that made up the old double bill. And all the mustachioed riders of the sage have given way to the relentless advance of screen progress. It is our loss.

New Legends

Are today's baseball players as good as yesterday's? Is O. J. Simpson as good a football player as Red Grange? Could Jim Thorpe run today's Olympic athletes into the ground? Does the current crop of movie tough guys stack up well against the screen greats of Hollywood's golden era?

Those are four unanswerable questions. In the case of the athletes, it is obvious that sports have changed so much over the years that direct comparison is impossible. Even high school runners today can better some of the records Jim Thorpe set. Less obviously, the movies have changed so much that comparing tough guys of different eras is no easy job, even though we have a lasting record on film. The number of movies being made has gone way down, audience attitudes have changed from the comparative innocence of old to a shock-resistant sophistication, and the rigid movie code of morals has given way to an often shocking acceptance of brutality and evil.

But there is still one constant: the movies need stars —especially tough guys. The movies don't necessarily need good actors to fill the bill. Good acting seems incidental to that elusive characteristic called star quality— the ability to project a personality that somehow wins the audience. You often can't predict who has star quality. The audiences decide the question on the basis of feeling rather than logic.

Few of his fans would describe Charles Bronson as a great actor. Many would agree that he is far from handsome in the conventional meaning of the word. If you look closely at the plots of some of Bronson's biggest hits, such as *The Valachi Papers* and *The Stone Killers,* you see all sorts of weaknesses and illogicalities. But people pay money to see Charles Bronson movies. His image is simple, manly and straight, the kind you would expect from his coal-mining past. And apparently, that image is enough to put Bronson among the highest-paid stars in Hollywood history. While film critics of the 1970s were turning thumbs down on Bronson and praising sensitive, obscure psychological dramas, Bronson was being paid $1.5 million a film and a percentage of the profits. That's star quality, tough-guy style.

You find the same brand of star quality in an actor

who was an unlikely candidate for stardom, Bruce Lee. It was difficult to call Lee an actor at all, and it was difficult to judge his films by any conventional standard. All that Bruce Lee had to offer was some flashing demonstrations of the oriental martial arts; all that his films had to offer was the monotonous spectacle of good guy Bruce cutting down legions of bad guys with karate chops and quick kicks.

Lee's premature death at the age of thirty-two eliminated any chance of finding out whether he had more to offer than was evident in his brief screen history. Nevertheless, people came out in force to see the films, and movie makers soon were gathering up every scrap of Bruce Lee footage to take advantage of his popularity. You can give Lee most of the credit for the series of martial-arts films that became a fad in the early 1970s. The fad faded, and the fading was faster because none of the actors who followed in Lee's footsteps had his star quality.

A fad of slightly more durability was started by Sean Connery, who had knocked around in films for a while with no special distinction when he hit the jackpot as James Bond, the British superspy whose code number was 007 and whose ability to rub out any number of spies, to master any piece of complex electronic equipment and to charm any beautiful woman on sight was irresistible to audiences. The first James Bond film was *Dr. No,* made in 1963, which astonished its makers by the box office bonanza it created. (Incidentally, Dr. No, the wily wizard who was out to conquer the world, was played by Joseph Wiseman, a sharp-faced villain who has been impressive in the relatively few movies he has made.)

As soon as the producers recovered from their shock, they realized that they had a sure-fire formula on their hands: plenty of scantily clad beauties, all of whom were fair game for secret agent Bond; plenty of blood as minor hirelings of master criminals fell by the score; and plenty of far-out inventions, like folding helicopters and rocket sleds. After *Dr. No,* it was *From Russia with Love, Goldfinger, Thunderball* and *You Only Live Twice.*

The James Bond movies raked in the money and Sean Connery's fees got bigger and bigger. Before long, most people thought that James Bond and Sean Connery were indistinguishable. But Connery was getting increasingly restless. As he did more Bond films, he kept insisting that he could really act if he had a chance—a proposition that seemed unlikely, considering his undistinguished career in pre-Bond days and the lackluster nature of one or two films he made in between the Bond sagas.

However, Connery had the last laugh. Walking away from the Bond image, he began to do some real acting in such films as *The Molly Maguires* and *The Anderson Tapes.* After being wooed back by an irresistible offer for one last James Bond appearance, in *Diamonds Are Forever,* Connery settled down to real acting. Shedding the smoothness of the Bond character, he still could let his ruggedness show through. Even more impressive, he could make the transition from ordinary tough-guy roles to middle age on the screen. In a movie

THUNDERBALL

Sean Connery in a typical James Bond pose: a beautiful
woman in one hand, a weapon in the other.
(*United Artists, 1965*)

like *Murder on the Orient Express,* Connery could let his graying hair and growing paunch be evident without losing his appeal.

By then, the flood of James Bond imitations had begun to dwindle. It would be hard to list all the actors who had a try at imitating Sean Connery, either in single movies or in series. Only a couple of actors can be remembered very well. One was Dean Martin as superspy Matt Helm in *Murderers' Row* and a couple of other films that added nothing to the sex-and-technology formula. Somehow, the sleepy-eyed, definitely untough Martin managed to be at least half convincing as a man who could outfight any villain on the planet.

More convincing was James Coburn, as *Our Man Flint* and a sequel, *In Like Flint.* Coburn was more your idea of a tough guy—rawboned, sharp-eyed, with a menacing grin. In Britain, it was Michael Caine, with a cockney accent and eyeglasses, playing a more vulnerable spy named Harry Palmer in *The Ipcress File, Funeral in Berlin* and *Billion Dollar Brain.*

Most of the Bond-type spy movies of the 1960s have aged badly. There are just so many special effects tricks that can be pulled on the screen and just so many bikini-wearing women who can be run through a movie without creating boredom. The spy-movie fad was fun while it lasted, but there wasn't much in the way of memorable tough guys to show for it when it was over.

One coming star who didn't get sucked into the James Bond machine was Steve McQueen, who has turned out to be one of the great tough guys of the

1970s. McQueen was unusual in one respect: He became successful in the movies after first making his name on television. Not too many stars have moved from the small tube to the big screen, but McQueen did it by first starring in a successful television series, "Wanted—Dead or Alive," and then moving on to top roles in Hollywood.

McQueen is a symbol of the times in another way: When you think of him, you tend to think of wheels. In his first really big starring role, as one of the prisoners of war in *The Great Escape,* his most memorable scenes were on a motorcycle (as it happens, McQueen is a dedicated motorcyclist off the screen). In another of his best parts, the title role in the tough detective story, *Bullitt,* the biggest scene is a carefully choreographed auto chase that goes up and down the hills of San Francisco and ends in flaming death.

It was natural that McQueen would play a racing driver in *Le Mans,* and that he would appear in a documentary on motorcycling, *Any Sunday.* It seems safe to assume that audiences will be seeing more of Steve McQueen on wheels in the future.

It is interesting to contrast McQueen with another major star of the 1970s, Robert Redford. McQueen is an authentic tough guy of the old school, a tight, compressed, narrow-eyed ball of tension waiting to explode, a man moving on wheels in a roar of power. Redford is a smoother, softer character. He moves on skis (as in *Downhill Racer*) or on foot in the wilderness (as in *Jeremiah Johnson*).

McQueen can play a cop like Bullitt and appear to

BULLITT

Steve McQueen clears a crowded airport waiting room as he
hunts down the villain in the climactic scene.
(*Warner Brothers, 1968*)

be illegally tough. Redford can play a con man, in *The Sting,* or even a Western gunfighter, in *Butch Cassidy and the Sundance Kid,* and appear to be having light-hearted fun even as he bilks someone of big wads of money or comes out of a bank with guns blazing. If you want to make comparisons with past stars, McQueen recalls the old James Cagney, minus the dancing quality, while Redford can be described as sort of a corn-fed Errol Flynn.

Or maybe it is best to say that Redford is more like Robert Mitchum, minus some of Mitchum's taut toughness. One difference between the two is that Redford achieved stardom, riches and adulation almost overnight and without appearing to try very hard, while Mitchum had to labor for years in the movies to get the credit that was due to him.

Mitchum broke into the movies in the early 1940s, and not spectacularly. In fact, he was one of the subsidiary bad guys in the Westerns. You can find Mitchum's name down low in the billing of some Hopalong Cassidy movies, usually as one of the heavies. He began to work his way up the ladder, getting larger parts and more notices in everything from comedies (he was in Laurel and Hardy's *Dancing Masters*) to wartime morale boosters like *Gung Ho!* and *Thirty Seconds Over Tokyo.*

But Mitchum really hit it big when he was chosen to play the part of a platoon officer in *The Story of G. I. Joe,* a war film based on the war experiences of correspondent Ernie Pyle. *G. I. Joe* was unusual because it tried to show what combat really was like for the front-line soldier—the mud, the monotony, the constant presence of death. In the final, moving scene, the body of the platoon leader is brought down a hill on a mule. His men, one by one, say a word of good-bye before they slog off to more fighting. Sleepy-eyed and casual, Mitchum yet was a convincing combat leader.

He didn't get many parts that good over the next few years, although he kept busy in starring roles. Typically, he was the tough guy hero playing opposite sultry leading women such as Jane Russell or Lizabeth Scott in films with titles like *His Kind of Woman, The Racket* and *Macao.* Given that kind of success—the films usually got bad reviews but made plenty of money —it was easy to write Mitchum off as just another hunk of Hollywood beefcake who got by on his physique, not his acting ability. (Another actor who had that reputation was Victor Mature, who reportedly told a director who asked him for more expression during one scene, "I have two expressions, full face and profile. Which do you want?")

But Mitchum could act. He was chilling in *The Night of the Hunter,* a 1955 thriller that had him playing the off-beat part of a psychopathic country preacher out to kill two children who knew he had murdered their mother. If critics didn't appreciate Mitchum, audiences and directors did. Over the years, he has acted for most of the great directors in Hollywood, almost invariably winning their praise for his professionalism and his lack of superstar ego.

Mitchum has the ability to make a borderline movie look good, as he did in a routine Western called *Bandido,* and a good movie look better, as he did in the excellent Howard Hawks Western, *El Dorado.* Mit-

HIS KIND OF WOMAN

Robert Mitchum is on the receiving end
and Raymond Burr is the gunman.
(*RKO, 1951*)

chum is still acting, and there are predictions that the next big Bogart-type fan cult will be built around his quiet but penetrating screen presence.

Mitchum isn't the only recent candidate for cultdom. There is also Burt Lancaster, who also made his appearance in films in the 1940s and grew steadily in acting range after that. Burt Lancaster started by being able to portray a more muscular toughness than Mitchum did. Lancaster's first two important roles set the pattern. He was Swede, a prize fighter turned gangster, in *The Killers,* a 1946 movie based loosely on an Ernest Hemingway short story. And he was a hard-as-nails convict in a brutal prison film, *Brute Force,* the next year.

After a few more films of that sort (*Rope of Sand, Criss Cross*), Lancaster turned to swashbucklers. He had been a circus acrobat for a time, and he recruited an old circus partner named Nick Cravat for a few tongue-in-cheek costume adventures that featured a lot of swinging from rafters, tumbling off roofs and on-the-run duels. But serious parts followed: a middle-aged doctor fighting against alcoholism in *Come Back, Little Sheba,* the top sergeant in a tough-minded film about the prewar army, *From Here to Eternity,* and the main character of the film version of *The Rose Tattoo,* a Tennessee Williams play.

You can say that Lancaster has more or less alternated acting roles and tough-guy roles: first a gunfighter in *Gunfight at the O K Corral* and then a vicious Broadway columnist in *The Sweet Smell of Success;* another Western, *The Unforgiven,* followed by an

BRUTE FORCE

Charles Bickford is the fatherly con who seems to have
his doubts about the angelic air of Burt Lancaster.
(*Universal, 1947*)

Oscar-winning portrayal of a conniving, dishonest evangelist in *Elmer Gantry*. One of his better roles wrapped up the two parts of Lancaster in one role: *Bird Man of Alcatraz,* the true story of a convicted killer who made himself into one of the world's leading experts on bird behavior by studying in his prison cell. Burt Lancaster could show you both the violence in the killer and the inner strength of the imprisoned, self-made scholar.

Lancaster is a tough guy with more than one dimension. Who else but Burt Lancaster could play the proud head of a nineteenth-century aristocratic family (in *The Leopard,* 1963) and a dedicated professional working to train retarded children (in *A Child is Waiting*) the same year? Lancaster still is adding to his screen record, but it is one of the most interesting and rewarding to have come out of Hollywood in any era.

Kirk Douglas made his debut in films the same year as Burt Lancaster (1946), but with a different personality. While Lancaster started out playing muscular toughness, Douglas started out playing sneaky toughness. His first part was as the alcoholic husband of Barbara Stanwyck in *The Strange Love of Martha Ivers*. He quickly played a hoodlum chief who bedeviled Robert Mitchum in *Out of the Past* and scored his first major success as the absolutely rotten, scheming prizefighter who clawed his way to the top in *Champion*. Rottenness seemed to become a basic part of the Douglas screen character. He was a dishonest newspaper reporter in *The Big Carnival,* a hysterically brutal policeman in *Detective Story,* an out-and-out heel of a movie producer in *The Bad and the Beautiful*.

But there was more in Douglas than just tough crooks. In 1956, he scored an artistic success playing Vincent van Gogh in *Lust for Life,* a lushly produced and respectful biography of the artist. Alas, the film died at the box office. But the next year Douglas was excellent in the grim role of a French World War I infantry officer in *Paths of Glory,* which many critics consider to be the best antiwar movie made in Hollywood in recent decades.

The film told the story of a French army unit that was sent to certain death against an impregnable enemy position merely because some generals wanted to win medals and promotion. As Colonel Dax, the one honest officer in this sordid affair, Douglas had to be the image of honesty and integrity. And he was. Kirk Douglas has had his ups and downs since then—ups such as his effective work as a cowboy seeking freedom in the bureaucratic modern world in *Lonely Are the Brave* (with Walter Matthau doing equally well as the Western sheriff who was chasing Douglas); and downs such as a brief appearance in a flop suspense story, *The List of Adrian Messenger.* But Douglas has established his place as one of the true big stars of the postwar years.

Another Douglas deserves some mention here—Paul Douglas, who got started late in the movies and had an unhappily short career, but belongs on any true list of movie tough guys. Paul Douglas was a good-natured tough guy, more at home in comedies than in action films. He would have had a better film career if he had not made a mistake by turning down the first part that

PATHS OF GLORY
Kirk Douglas is the hard-bitten French officer
in this disillusioned view of war.
(*United Artists, 1957*)

was offered to him. First a radio announcer and then a straight man to Jack Benny in the radio era, Paul Douglas made his real acting debut in the Broadway play *Born Yesterday,* about a loud-mouthed junkyard millionaire who eventually is defeated by his bubble-headed girl friend (played by that wonderful comedienne, Judy Holliday). Douglas turned down the chance to act the same part on the screen, but he did accept a role as a loud-mouthed department store millionaire in *A Letter to Three Wives,* a fine 1949 comedy.

From then on, Douglas played pretty much the same part in every movie—the burly he-man, a loud shouter but sentimental at the core, who talked tough but could be counted on to do the right thing. Maybe the best of those parts was in *Panic In the Streets,* in which Douglas played a New Orleans detective who slowly came to the realization that there was a real urgency to track down a killer to prevent an epidemic of black plague. But almost as good was his role as a loud-mouthed business executive who was won over by a stockholder (his old friend Judy Holliday again) in *The Solid Gold Cadillac.* Paul Douglas died of a heart attack at a young age, and he is missed.

However, a lot of old-film fans sometimes have difficulty distinguishing between Paul Douglas and another actor of roughly the same age and type, Broderick Crawford. The confusion is compounded because it was Crawford who played on the screen the *Born Yesterday* role that Douglas made famous on stage. The difference between Douglas and Crawford is that Crawford somehow lacks a sense of humor on the screen. He comes on harder and more menacing than Paul Douglas ever could.

It is significant that Douglas won an Oscar playing an unsympathetic, basically villainous role—the Southern demagogue, modeled after Huey Long, in *All the King's Men*. Douglas never really played a screen villain, and Crawford played hardly anything else (his role in *Born Yesterday* was the big exception). Always a reliable actor, Crawford has seldom been a great one, but he can be depended upon to add a genuine note of toughness when it is needed.

After all of this, can anyone say who the next great tough guy of the movies will be? Not really, because they have a way of appearing without notice. However, there is a new possibility that has been created by developments in the movie world in recent years; the next tough guy may well come from overseas. After all, even though Charles Bronson is American-born, his stardom was a product of European-made films. And we even have an example of one foreign film star who has made a name for himself almost entirely as the result of foreign films.

The star is Toshiro Mifune, who has made a series of swashbuckling samurai films with Akira Kurosawa as the director. Made in Japan and based on Japanese history, these films have achieved world-wide distribution and have been paid the sincerest form of film compliment: imitation. *The Magnificent Seven,* an American Western that starred Yul Brynner and Steve McQueen among others, was nothing but an English-language remake of Kurosawa's *Seven Samurai.*

THE FRENCH CONNECTION
Gene Hackman dodges bullets as Popeye
Doyle, the tough New York detective.
(*20th Century-Fox, 1971*)

THE GODFATHER

Al Pacino, Marlon Brando, James Caan and John Cazale. It's a long way from *Little Caesar* to this smooth image of gangland. (*Paramount, 1972*)

In the samurai movies, as in American Westerns, the hero is a laconic stranger who comes into a town at war and tames it by his heroic deeds. In the samurai film, the hero is on foot and uses a sword to cut down the evil opponents, but the basic plot is the same as that of the conventional Western. Kurosawa did well enough in Japanese films so that he was invited to Europe to film a Western with one of the strangest international casts on record—Alain Delon from France, Charles Bronson from the United States, Mifune from Japan, just to name a few. But the film did not succeed and Mifune made no others in the West.

A Japanese tough guy as an American hero seems improbable, but how about a French tough guy? For a while in the 1960s, it seemed as if Jean-Paul Belmondo was in the running. Or a British tough guy? It's a small world these days, and almost anything is possible. One thing is just about certain. More screen tough guys are coming along, because without them the movies wouldn't be the same.

Who can forget Gene Hackman as the tough-as-nails New York cop, Popeye Doyle, in *The French Connection* and its sequel, unimaginatively called *French Connection II*. Hackman in these films is tough in the style of the 1970s—unromantic, gritty, as much a loser as a winner. For a smoother form of toughness, there was Al Pacino in *The Godfather* and its inevitable sequel. It was typical of our times that Pacino's sophisticated gangster appeared more sympathetic than Hackman's rough, ugly cop. Movie toughness is changing, but there's as much of it as ever.

DINNER AT EIGHT

Who could look more wicked than
Jean Harlow does amid all the luxury?
(*MGM, 1933*)

Tough Gals

Most heroines of the screen have been in the pattern set by those two great early stars, Lillian Gish and Mary Pickford—fragile flowers, beautiful to look at but easily bruised and requiring the protection of strong men. But a few screen actresses have broken out of that mold to create characters every bit as tough as the Bogarts and the Cagneys. The ratio of tough gals to fragile flowers is definitely low—at least ten flowers to every tough gal—but the exceptions to the rule have helped make movies much livelier than they would have been otherwise.

There was Jean Harlow, the platinum blonde of the 1930s, who projected an image that was raucous, hard and captivating. You can get an idea of the sort of role played by Harlow by just running over the titles of some of her hit movies: *Red-Headed Woman, Bombshell, Riffraff, Libeled Lady, Wife vs. Secretary.* Harlow was no delicate flower and she was not someone who would sit still and let a grapefruit be pushed in her face. Very clearly, she was as tough in her own way as any actor in any of her films.

In particular, she showed that she was the ideal co-star for Clark Gable, the unquestioned he-man king of the screen, with whom she made *Red Dust, China Seas,* and several other films. Jean Harlow never had a chance to grow old. She died in 1937 of an infection, just twenty-six years old but already a screen legend that lives on today.

Only a handful of actresses can be ranked with Jean Harlow for screen toughness. Bette Davis is one of them. Or maybe it would be better to say that Bette Davis is one of a kind. Jean Harlow made it in films because of her slinkiness and brassy good looks. Bette Davis was never really good-looking, at least not in the full-blown, obvious way that Hollywood usually demands of starlets. She made it because she was an actress who could convey a sort of high-strung toughness, mixed with vulnerability, that was all her very own.

Melodrama is the natural style of Bette Davis. She always seems to be playing a woman fighting against the odds, often ruthlessly. Her first really big role, the one that made her famous, was as a scheming cockney gold-digger trying to ruin the life of Leslie Howard in *Of Human Bondage,* made in 1934. After that, it was films with titles like *Front Page Woman* and *Danger-*

ous, both made in 1935 (she won an Oscar for *Danger-ous* and, in 1938, another one for *Jezebel*).

The movies worked their stars hard in those days. In 1936, Bette Davis was in three films, *The Petrified Forest, The Golden Arrow* and *Satan Met a Lady*. After that last film (which was, incidentally, a very bad film version of *The Maltese Falcon,* Dashiell Hammett's novel), she walked out on her contract with Warner Brothers, saying that the roles they were giving her were inferior, and sailed off to London to make a movie without the studio's permission. The studio sued and won in court, but she won the real fight because her parts got noticeably better. The episode was a flash of off-screen fire that showed what was really behind the screen image.

It would take pages to list all the movies that Bette Davis made in her peak years. She had enough great parts—or parts that she made great—to satisfy half a dozen lesser actresses. She was the unfaithful wife who shot down her lover in *The Letter;* the scheming, villainous daughter of a decadent Southern family in *The Little Foxes;* a brittle, spoiled, doomed rich girl in *Dark Victory;* and twins, one good and one bad, in *A Stolen Life.*

In 1950 she summed it all up in *All About Eve,* in which she played an aging Broadway star who was obviously nervous about growing old and who was taken in by a scheming younger actress. It was a marvelous comedy, and the only thing wrong with it was that Anne Baxter, who played the younger actress, was obviously no match for Bette Davis in scheming.

JEZEBEL

Bette Davis in full flower as a wicked belle of
the Old South. Henry Fonda is her beau.
(*Warner Brothers, 1938*)

A lot of older actresses fade away. Bette Davis has gone into horror-type films in which she almost parodies her earlier screen roles. In films like *Hush . . . Hush, Sweet Charlotte* and *What Ever Happened to Baby Jane?* everything has been turned up a notch or two, so that the merely nervous roles of old have become hysterical, and the violence that was implied now is splattered in blood across the screen. When you think about it, it seems appropriate. Would anyone expect a tough gal like Bette Davis to grow old gracefully?

What Ever Happened to Baby Jane? brought Bette Davis together with another memorable star of Hollywood's golden era, Joan Crawford, who had her own brand of screen toughness. Joan Crawford broke into movies in the 1920s as a dancing flapper. Just to give you an idea of how the movies operated in those days, her studio ran a magazine contest to give her a screen name (she was born Lucille Le Sueur in Texas). In the 1930s, she stopped dancing and had a long string of roles in which she was a career girl who suffered because of love—*Today We Live, I Live My Life, The Last of Mrs. Cheyney,* and so on. In the 1940s, she became the middle-aged woman who was having a tough time, often with younger men, in films such as *Humoresque, Possessed, Daisy Kenyon* and *Mildred Pierce,* for which she won an Oscar. In the 1960s, it was horror-type movies à la Bette Davis—*Strait Jacket, I Saw What You Did*—in which hysteria was the keynote. She retired in the 1960s, firmly established as a screen legend, and died in 1977.

One actress who never quite made it to the very top

was Mary Astor, whom we met in *The Maltese Falcon* at the beginning of this book. That one role established Mary Astor's credentials as both an excellent actress and someone who could match Humphrey Bogart for screen toughness. But by that time, it was already later in Mary Astor's screen career than anyone knew. She had been in films since the 1920s and made the transition to sound from the silent era successfully.

The titles of her 1930s films give the best idea of the sort of role she played: *Other Men's Women, Smart Woman, I Am a Thief.* It was natural that she would be the hard-as-nails Brigid O'Shaughnessy in *The Maltese Falcon,* and she had a run of good parts in the early 1940s, winning an Oscar playing opposite Bette Davis in *The Great Lie* (1941). But then, as she acknowledged later in her autobiography, personal problems caught up with her and her screen roles tailed off. Mary Astor didn't reach the heights that she was capable of attaining, but her screen achievements still are impressive.

It is curious to note how many careers of screen tough gals intersected with that of Humphrey Bogart— Bette Davis, Mary Astor and, most emphatically, Lauren Bacall. In fact, Lauren Bacall's best screen work seems to have been the films she did with Bogart when she first broke into the movies. Her screen debut came in 1944 opposite Bogart in *To Have and Have Not,* based on a Hemingway story. She later starred with Bogart in *The Big Sleep* and *Key Largo;* by then they were married.

After Bogart's death, Lauren Bacall slowly made a

WHAT EVER HAPPENED TO BABY JANE?

Bette Davis, gritty to the end, playing a grisly parody
of her old self with another old trouper, Joan Crawford.
(*Warner Brothers, 1962*)

transition from playing tough parts in detective stories to playing light roles in musicals and comedies. She seemed to lose interest in the screen; her appearance in *Murder on the Orient Express* in 1974 was her first film role in eight years. The combination of Bacall and Bogart seems to have been a unique kind of film chemistry. Even today, with those movies far behind her, people are still imitating that moment in her first film when she looked at Bogart and said, in her own inimitable way, "If you want me, just whistle. You know how to whistle, don't you? You just pucker your lips—and blow." Careers have been built on less than those lines.

And how could any book ignore the one and only Tallulah Bankhead, a marvelously gifted actress with a husky voice that should have been patented and a genius for picking lousy parts. Tallulah made only a few pictures, most of them bad, during a long acting career. One exception was *Lifeboat,* Alfred Hitchcock's improbable drama set in an open boat. And that was about it. It's fun to watch Tallulah rumble and thunder when one of her rare films gets an occasional revival, but it's a shame to think of what she could have done in the movies if she had set her mind to it.

No apologies are needed for Marlene Dietrich, whose screen career seems to be eternal. She started in Germany in 1930 as the wicked night-club singer, Lola-Lola, in *The Blue Angel,* and flourished in a series of shady-lady screen roles for more than thirty years. Perhaps the essence of Marlene Dietrich's film personality was expressed in a movie called *Shanghai Express,* a florid 1932 melodrama set in China, in which she looked at Clive Brook, a British actor playing a man from her past who still loved her, and said in that husky, lisping voice, "It took more than one man to change my name to Shanghai Lilly." It was pure corn, made believable by the way Dietrich said it.

In the Hollywood of the 1930s, actresses were divided into Good Girls and Bad Girls. The Good Girls usually were demure brunettes who acted shy and won the good guy in the end. The Bad Girls were blondes who generally made an open play for the hero and usually (a) gave him up out of sheer self-sacrifice or (b) died conveniently at the end, often in a hail of bullets, so the hero could marry the Good Girl. Marlene Dietrich was the best Bad Girl of them all, in films such as *Dishonored, Blonde Venus, The Scarlet Empress* and *Rancho Notorious.*

She isn't on the screen any more, but her presence lingers on. In *Blazing Saddles,* Mel Brooks' grossly vulgar parody of every Western ever made, Madeline Kahn's role is nothing but an all-out imitation of Marlene Dietrich. (The Dietrich role that was being imitated came from *Destry Rides Again,* in which Marlene was the saloon singer who fell in love with good guy James Stewart and died tearily in the end.)

Ida Lupino is another tough gal of the 1930s and the 1940s who is worth a second look because of her success in cracking the previous all-male world of film directing. In most of her film roles, Ida Lupino played gun molls or their equivalent—hard if not brassy women in films such as *They Drive by Night* and *Escape Me*

Never. Always a competent actress, she never hit the real heights. But her ability to become a film director in the late 1940s and 1950s, when no other woman could break into the top ranks of Hollywood, speaks for the personal drive that was behind the screen image. Ida Lupino was ahead of the times and a portent of things to come.

Some other screen tough gals deserve mention: Rosalind Russell, who seemed to have played only hard-boiled career women in man-tailored suits (it was entirely appropriate that when Hollywood made a film version of *The Front Page* called *His Gal Friday,* Rosalind Russell would play the previously male part of ace reporter Hildy Johnson; most of the dialogue remained the same and they didn't even change the name of the character). Then there was Ann Sheridan, the perpetual tough-minded woman up against the hard realities of life, playing opposite Cagney in *Angels With Dirty Faces,* opposite Bogart in *They Drive by Night* and opposite Garfield in *They Made Me a Criminal.* And Judith Anderson, who specialized in playing older shrews, most memorably as the villainous Eudora on the "Bewitched" TV series.

And we can't forget Barbara Stanwyck, who played alternate roles as tough, ruthless women and tender victims in films and then went on to a successful television career. One role above all stamps Barbara Stanwyck as a great screen tough gal: the scheming wife leading Fred MacMurray into murder for money and love in *Double Indemnity,* a 1944 Billy Wilder suspense movie that still has not lost its sting. And there is Shelley

Winters, who has veered from brassiness to vulnerability in a screen career that is best described as checkered.

So who is going to occupy the niche established by these tough gals? There are any number of candidates. Faye Dunaway's beauty has not prevented her from projecting a 1970s-style toughness in films such as *Bonnie and Clyde, Chinatown* and *Network,* in which many of the evils that movies once only hinted about are now thrown openly onto the screen. There is Jane Fonda, who started out as just another screen starlet and has worked her way to painfully realistic roles in such films as *They Shoot Horses, Don't They?* and *Klute.* There is Shirley MacLaine, mostly a song-and-dance woman and a comedienne who has started to move into more serious roles. The tough roles for men on the screen haven't changed for decades. But things are changing for women in film. It's going to be interesting to see how Hollywood handles its women on the screen in the years ahead.

INDEX

Although EDWARD EDELSON spends most of his working hours as the science editor of the New York *Daily News,* he still manages to find time to watch plenty of old movies. A graduate of New York University and a Sloan-Rockefeller Fellow in the Advanced Science Writing Program at Columbia University, Mr. Edelson now lives in Jamaica, New York, with his wife and three children. His previous books include *Great Monsters of the Movies, The Book of Prophecy, Visions of Tomorrow: Great Science Fiction from the Movies, Funny Men of the Movies,* and *Great Movie Spectaculars.*